A Strong Life

Stories of the humor and humanity of some of the characters who have lived and worked in Strong and other small Maine towns

by **Richard A. Bean Sr.**

Cover image
and interior illustrations by Craig A. Delorme
Photos on pages 6, 9, 143 and 209 from
Strong, Maine—Incorporated 1801
Layout by Laura Ashton, laura@gitflorida.com

Copyright ©2011 by Richard A Bean Sr.

Although some of the characters is this book are real, most of their names (except Roy and Mabel Lewis, and Cousin Arthur) were changed to protect their privacy.

Second Printing

ISBN: 978-0-9845898-4-5

Printed in the United States of America

PRGott Books Publishing
P O Box 43
Norway, Maine 04268

www.prgottbooks.net

Other books by Richard A Bean Sr.

The Struggle

Dedication and Acknowledgements

Dedicated to my dear daughter Judy Lewis, who assumed all the details associated with the computer and emailing.

I also wish to acknowledge:

Liz Mockler, a dear friend who did a lot of the editing and rewriting.

Craig DeLorme, a dear best-friend and talented cartoonist who enhanced the pages of this book with his illustrations.

Tracy, Dee, Nicole, and Mrs. Huntley, from Park Street Press in South Paris, Maine, who printed the multitude of drafts necessary for me to get this book written.

Debbie Crossman, a long-time friend, confidant, and supporter who has been a trusted critic of my writing.

And finally, my publisher who enhanced the pages of this book considerably.

I sincerely thank them all; without their help, this book could not have been completed

A Personal Note from the Author

The stories, comments, and opinions in this book are not intended to offend anyone or to make fun of, criticize, or demean anyone's beliefs, lifestyles, or personal circumstances.

They are, however, written to hopefully put a little humor in the lives of all who may read them—and perhaps a smile on their faces—as they recollect "characters" they have known in their own lives.

As for opinions and comments expressed by either the people I write about or by myself, it is hoped readers will remember they have their own and are entitled to them—regardless of whether or not we agree.

As one wise man once said, *"Opinions are like our personalities: We all have them, yet they are all different."* We do not have to agree or accept them. But if we respect them, we'll be just fine.

Richard A Bean Sr.

Contents

	Introduction	1
Chapter 1	**Back in the Day**	5
Chapter 2	**A Man Named Woodshed**	12
Chapter 3	**Charlie and his Not-So-Model-A**	18
Chapter 4	**Pearly, The Pig, and Santa**	21
Chapter 5	**The Untold Story of Silvo Packard**	28
Chapter 6	**The Wisdom of an Unnamed Character**	34
Chapter 7	**Changing Times**	38
Chapter 8	**The Great Depression of 1929**	42
Chapter 9	**More About Changes**	47
Chapter 10	**The Chainin' Gang**	51
Chapter 11	**Diapers, Duct Tape, and a Day with Grandpa**	60
Chapter 12	**Humming Along—Not!**	64
Chapter 13	**Happy Campers**	69
Chapter 14	**Who's the Boss**	73
Chapter 15	**Halloween Pranks from the Past**	78
Chapter 16	**The Rest of the Story**	85
Chapter 17	**The Story of Norman**	89
Chapter 18	**The Crazy Antics of a Guy Called Shrimp**	92
Chapter 19	**Kids Do the Darnedest Things**	96
Chapter 20	**Priceless Memories Never Before Told**	102
Chapter 21	**The Story of Clyde**	107

Chapter 22   The Delightful Stories of Ah-Ah and Dampy   112

Chapter 23   A Story for Children Who Don't Believe   116
                                      in Santa Claus

Chapter 24   Taken for Granted   120

Chapter 25   Woodshed Strikes Again   123

Chapter 26   More Thoughts About Friends   126

Chapter 27   The Story of a Pig Named Dolly   128

Chapter 28   The Story of Uncle Nelson   133

Chapter 29   One In and Out   139

Chapter 30   Roughing It   141

Chapter 31   Embarrassing Moments with a Friend   147

Chapter 32   The Other Side of the Story   153

Chapter 33   More Stories About Life in Strong   158

Chapter 34   The Murder of a Chainsaw   164

Chapter 35   Another Murder, This Time of a Choice   168
                                      Igloo Cooler

Chapter 36   The Rider of a Lifetime   172

Chapter 37   A Story About One of My (In)famous Ideas   177

Chapter 38   The Loyalty and Love of a Devoted Wife   184

Chapter 39   A Politician's Ideas and Philosophy   188

Chapter 40   Sense and Sensibility   191

Chapter 41   The Agreeable Farmer with the Unlucky Pig   195

Chapter 42   The Story of Walt   198

Chapter 43   No One Will Be Forgotten   202

Chapter 44   Roy Lewis' Drug Store   205

Chapter 45   The Potato Digger   211

             About the Author   214

A Strong Life

by **Richard A. Bean, Sr.**

Introduction

The town of Strong could easily be overlooked in the remote, rugged woods of the northwestern part of Maine. As its name implies, life in that deeply-forested region is a struggle for most people, yet they remained strong and stubbornly loyal to the meadows, mountains and farmland they call home.

The same was true in the late 1940s and 1950s, where I spent my most formative years and learned so much about the people who worked the woods and mills and built an unforgettable legacy of simple, honest traditions, hearty spirits, humor and an unequaled work ethic.

At the time of my youth, employment in Strong and other small woodland towns in Maine was nearly at 100 percent. There were two full-time woodworking mills, a bustling hotel owed by one of the mills, several stores, both grocery and convenience, and a full-time operating lumber sawmill where anyone who wanted work could find it.

Entering the main village from the south, visitors would find all of the stores and other businesses on one side of the street, and the post office, telephone central office and a few homes on the other.

There was a small grocery store, a barbershop,

a hardware store, and a clothing store, among other establishments. In short, it was quintessential Maine— and still remains so despite a devastating fire that leveled a major portion of the entire town in December 1969.

With all of the post World War II prosperity, Strong also had something else—its humorous characters and a few storytellers who could record and pass down some of the funny tales of everyday life in one of the most rugged areas of Maine.

To be considered a "character" in that part of the state, a person required some sort of individual distinction, quality, or habit. Not just anyone could be one. Lucky for us, there were plenty of Strong people who became rural legends in their time.

Although most all of the people written about in this anthology have passed, their memories and often-hilarious exploits are still as clear as a Maine lake in summer.

I strongly recommend (pun intended) that interested readers purchase a copy of *"Strong, Maine Incorporated 1801,"* a written history of the town published in 1992 and subtitled, in part, *"An historical account of a Sandy River settlement . . ."* The book may be purchased from the Strong Historical Society. It was authored by Lewis Brackley and Charles Lisherness and contains a vast amount of information about the town and its residents, including the story about the beloved town druggist, Royal "Roy" Lewis and his wife, Mabel— unquestionably two of the kindest and most endearing "characters" to ever call Strong home.

I also included the humorous story titled, "The Potato Digger," found on the final page of that historical account, which illustrates the humor of the people of Strong and the western region of Maine.

As you read my short stories on the people and way of life in Strong in the 1950s and 1960s, remember Roy Lewis's credo: *"Have a smile on your face, a whistle from your lips and a tune coming from your mouth."*

This positive attitude served him so well for so many years, and can do the same for anyone who gives it a try.

Chapter 1

Back in the Day

Although the introduction of this book talked a bit about the history of Strong, much was left unmentioned.

First, there was nothing said about Strong's school system or its athletic programs within the school or any of the other extracurricular activities that were so important to the town's children and families.

Missing, too, was the general layout of the bustling little town, as well as other details, which I think are important to fully understanding the life and times of Strong residents.

The shire town of Franklin County, Farmington, is 45 miles north of Lewiston and Auburn, Maine's second-largest urban region. Strong is about 10 miles northwest of Farmington, along the main Route 4.

To enter Strong village, it is necessary to veer right off of Route 4, which incidentally goes to Phillips, Madrid and on to Rangeley, Maine.

A short distance after leaving Route 4 into Strong, one would notice a gas station on the left and a baseball field on the right. Then in another short distance one would approach a bridge that crossed the Sandy River. Entering Strong from the south, one must cross this bridge. Once across, one would approach a fairly steep hill. Nearly at its top is a road to the right that intersects with the main road going into Strong.

Now, there are schools and then there are *schools*. The town's first school was a one-room school made of logs. A community privy was somewhere adjacent to the school. A playground with swings and teeter-totters also could be seen.

Later, a larger school was built to accommodate all 12 grade levels, plus kindergarten.

Old Strong Schoolhouse

There were three floors and a basement—half of which was dedicated to the custodians and their supplies, the furnace and the fuel storage. Once I reached high school age, I took the minimum four courses required each year in order to graduate. That was because even then, I was becoming an entrepreneur, which at the time I neither could pronounce or even understand its meaning.

In addition to working at the Strong Hotel during the week and helping Clyde, one of Strong's many "characters," I was also picking up discarded beer bottles along side the roads (and there were plenty) and cashing them in at Jack's, a beer store just beyond the Strong town line, since Strong was still a "dry town" in those earlier days.

In the fall, I would pick the so-called "drops" from a local apple orchard and take them to a mill to be squeezed into cider, which I sold door-to-door for 50 cents a gallon.

In-between picking bottles and apples, I would go to the drug store and get all the glass gallon jugs that were available—the owner liked my ambition and work ethic and saved me all the jugs he could. Back then, Coca-Cola syrup came in gallon jugs, much to my delight and profit. The druggist, or pharmacist as they are now called, would pour the syrup, or concentrated coke, in a soda glass and then add fizz, or seltzer water.

I would then take the jugs to the hotel basement laundry room for a thorough cleaning before filling them with fresh cider.

In addition, I also found a little time to chum with another friend, whose parents had a Model-A pickup truck and would travel to all the remote places where people dumped scrap iron, which included old cast iron cookware, parlor stoves and worn-out farm machinery.

We would then take the scrap iron to a Farmington junk dealer, who paid us well for our hard work.

Lest readers think I was a loser in high school, I must recognize my English teacher, who had a true passion for Shakespeare. Her tolerance of me was both unmatched and extraordinary and I learned much from her daily lessons.

A verse from Shakespeare might indeed describe her attitude toward me:

> *"Sweet are the uses of adversity,*
> *Which, like the toad, ugly and venomous,*
> *Wears yet a precious jewel in his head;*
> *And this our life, exempt from public haunt,*
> *Finds tongues in trees, books in running brooks,*
> *Sermons in stones, and good in everything."*

I would not change a moment of the time I was blessed to spend with that dedicated English teacher at Strong High School. Despite brain damage from being exposed to toxins later in life, and except for one small stanza, I can still recall today the entire Shakespeare quote I was taught by her more than six decades ago. The credit is due more to the teacher than to me.

Strong High School had its share of other school-related activities. Probably most interesting would be its basketball program, as this was from a time that can never be duplicated.

First, no parent today would accept the condition

of the facilities we used; secondly, today's teen-agers could never imagine using a Grange Hall as a gymnasium. Yet, that is precisely what we did. It was, after all, our only choice.

Strong Aurora Grange Hall

The basketball court was half the size of the courts today. Running through the walls, from side to side of the upstairs room, were two heavy metal rods with turnbuckles to keep the building from spreading.

These rods were located just above or slightly behind the foul line of the court, about eight feet or so off the floor. Eight to ten feet above the rods was the ceiling.

Basketball games were exciting—more so because we had to maneuver our shots between the rods and ceilings. Once in a while, if we were really lucky, the ball would strike the rod and bounce through the net, surprising everyone, most especially the shooter.

9

Moreover, without the thin full-sized mattresses that hung on the doors behind one of the hoops, I might have sustained brain injury far earlier in my life while attempting a simple lay-up shot.

On the opposite end of the court, the net hung over a stage that was used for plays, minstrel shows and concerts. Why none of us ever was seriously injured remains a mystery today.

Finally, in the middle of a frigid winter, someone would start stoking the wood furnaces at about 1 p.m. on the day of a game. Often, during the first half of the game, fans could still see their breath.

By half-time, most people would start shedding their mittens, scarves and, on a good night, even their coats. The principal was the boys' basketball coach and the school janitor coached the girls' team.

In 1951, town residents approved a plan to build a new school and a more modern gymnasium. But never did a basketball player in my time think he or she was being deprived in the old facilities. We were happy just to play.

While in high school, I was among the few boys who could boast of having his own car—thanks mostly to my numerous successful money-making ventures.

I found my first car sitting on a lawn I passed every time I went to the Grange Hall. After finding out there was little wrong with the car, I gleefully bought it and promptly found the Sears Roebuck catalogue and ordered four new tires for it, each costing $10. I also bought a battery for $6.

At about this same time, I started becoming interested in girls—something I was sure years earlier would never happen. Ah...to be so naïve again.

My first girlfriend was not only smart and beautiful, but she was an accomplished piano player as well. We were both each other's first love. Our relationship flourished and we married a few years after graduating from high school.

Yes, the "good old days" were indeed good to me and I am forever grateful for all the blessings I have enjoyed despite the struggles of my life.

Chapter 2

A Man Named "Woodshed"

This story is about a character affectionately called "Woodshed" and it should be understood first off that Woodshed was bestowed with the title of "character" for his many, many adventures—most of which ended innocently but badly.

Woodshed may have been one of my favorite characters. For certain, he was a true and loyal friend and our friendship is something I will always cherish.

Now, most everyone either knew or knows of a Woodshed. You recognize the type: somebody who really causes no harm to anyone, yet a person who can never seem to get much of anything quite right no matter how hard he tries. Woodshed was that kind of guy—and try he surely did.

He was a friendly chap, yet at times he could be downright cantankerous. Strangely, he was just the opposite of most fellows. That is to say, he was at his friendliest after visiting Jack's on the Avon town line, where he invariably put a couple of quarts of Ballantine ale under his belt. So, too, was he most friendly after he had gotten into his own "homemade spirits."

His cantankerous side would usually show when he

12

lost the body off the old 1931 Chevy coupe he insisted on driving.

There are a couple of other things that must be said before proceeding with Woodshed's story. First, he tended to be a little tight, or perhaps a better word would be "thrifty," when it came to spending money on his transportation.

Secondly, one must understand that in Woodshed's day it was perfectly acceptable—and legal—to drive around in a beat-up jalopy with the body held onto the frame with rope that Woodshed had salvaged from a farmer friend's barn hayfork.

Although Woodshed's actions were always well intended, there was a serious problem with his thriftiness when it came to his car. For instance, the salvaged rope was so wide that Woodshed couldn't get it wrapped tightly enough around the frame and up over the back side of the fenders and hood. Being somewhat ingenious, Woodshed punched two holes through the body just behind the front seat. This allowed him to get an extra wrap around the concoction to join the body and frame together.

Unfortunately, even that wasn't foolproof.

When it rained or when Woodshed took a corner at more than 30 miles-per-hour, the rope would stretch and off slid the body from the frame, leaving a trail of sparks and other items and debris in Woodshed's wake, such as candy wrappers, cigarette packages and an empty Ballantine bottle or two.

Finally, Woodshed realized that he must take more drastic measures. So he resorted to tying the rope completely over the top of the body and under the frame, then hooked his farmer friend's twitch horse to the rope to pull it tight. It was only after the rope began to crush the cab that Woodshed figured he had it tight enough.

This idea produced much better results, but unfortunately for Woodshed, the doors were tied so tight he now had to get in and out the windows.

With one problem solved, Woodshed always seemed to have another waiting close by. The jalopy tended to have a problem with the engine over-heating,

which required him to stop every 10 miles or so, find a stream, brook or bog and fill the radiator with a 10-quart pail he carried behind his seat. This, too, became troublesome, especially in the spring. Often times he would scoop up a bunch of frogs' eggs with the water and, because it was impossible to keep the radiator cap on, the eggs would boil out of the radiator and pepper the windshield before he could get to the next water hole.

Woodshed found that by using one of his empty quart Ballantine bottles he could filter out most of the eggs, so he had finally solved another problem.

For anyone who either lives in Strong or a small town like Strong, imagine if you will a 1931 Chevrolet "junker" making its way through town with half of the frame exposed and the body cocked sideways. And as though that was not odd enough, the radiator would be streaming like a geyser that looked like Old Faithful and the windshield would be plastered with pieces of grass, cooked frogs' eggs and anything else that might have been picked up since the last water hole.

Yup, people sure knew when Woodshed was coming through town.

Now, one would think Woodshed's jalopy and the ordeals he endured just to keep it on the road was what made him a character. Well, it did contribute to that honor, but not entirely. It also was Woodshed's drinking binges, his constant exaggeration of the truth, and the company he kept that set him apart from most other Strong folks.

And, yes, it must not be overlooked that Woodshed had a terrible stuttering problem—except when he was drinking. Once a quart or two of Ballantine or Pickwick ale found their destination into his belly, he was able to talk as good as you or me.

That's how Woodshed's friends or the other people close to him could tell when he'd been into the sauce, so to speak. But Woodshed, like most characters, was no dummy. He soon realized that the more he drank the better he talked. He also realized he could be drunker than a skunk and pretend to stutter and people would think he was sober.

This skill—if it could be called that—worked all well and good for most situations that Woodshed got himself into. Except the one that made him a true and genuine character. It also is how he got his nickname.

You see, one night Woodshed had been out drinking with some of his buddies and showed up at home later than usual from work. While explaining to his wife the reasons for his tardiness, he tried to fake his stuttering problem by telling her he had to work overtime.

"Well then," Sadie fired back, "you'd better call your boss back 'cause for the last three hours he's been callin' you to work a little overtime."

With that said, Woodshed muttered under his breath, "D-D-Dang f-f-foreman a-a-anyway," then did an about face and headed for the woodshed where he'd spend the remainder of that night—and probably the next three or four, especially if Woodshed's wife lived up to her reputation.

Chapter 3

Charlie and His Not-So-Model-A

Charlie was a hard-working Maine farmer, but he wasn't all that keen on personal hygiene. A daily bath or, for that matter, a weekly bath just wasn't part of his way of living.

Now, one could go on and on about Charlie's personal appearance, but that wouldn't be the special trademark that made him a character. No siree, his trademark was his most prized possession—a 1929 Model-A two-door sedan.

Charlie's Model-A may have been the only two-toned car around back in his day. As most know, until the 1930s, most if not all Model-A cars were made and shipped from the factory in one color: Jet black.

But not Charlie's Model-A; it definitely was a one of a kind.

Oh, it was black all right, but from just below the driver's side window running all the way back to the rear fender were unmistakable brown streaks that covered the entire side of the car.

But that wasn't all. Even the driver's side window, when rolled up, presented itself with the same dull shade of brown. With one exception. The brown streaks on the inside of the window were vertical so when looking at the car from a distance the whole car gave off a pleasant appearance of a two-toned look.

It was as though someone had taken great pains to get the colors coordinated just right and evenly distributed along the car's body.

But for strangers or someone who didn't know Charlie, the fact that the car was only two-toned on one side created somewhat of a mystery. Until, of course, they came forward for a closer inspection. You see, Charlie had a habit that contributed to his unique work of art. It was known as Red Man chewing tobacco. When Charlie piled a half pouch of this delicacy inside of his jowls the juices really began to take hold. In fact, the tobacco was so juicy that Charlie always gave his car a fresh coat of a "spider web" mural during his weekly trips to town. The car sure was a beauty from a distance.

Whenever this story was being told to strangers or to someone who didn't know Charlie well, the same question would always be asked: "But what about the vertical stains on the inside of the window?"

The answer, like the question, was always the same: "Oh yes, that's 'cause Charlie was a little absent-minded and he would forget to roll the widow down before he unloaded."

Chapter 4

Pearly, The Pig, and Santa

Pearly was known as one of the "good guys" in Strong. Not only was he a nice fellow, but he also was a good citizen. Still, Pearly had some unique qualities that qualified him as a character.

On one of my last visits to Pearly in the early 1950s, it was a sunny Sunday afternoon and I found him sitting in his favorite Boston rocker on his front porch. After our usual manly handshake and awkward hug, we got down to talking about the important things going on in Pearly's life—the pig and the garden he was raising, something he had done for the past 30 or so years.

Pearly could raise pigs and gardens like no one else I knew before or after. His pigs would always weigh in at more than 600 pounds at butchering time and his garden produced enough vegetables to feed half the town.

When I asked Pearly how he did it, he kept no secrets. "First, let your plants and pigs know that you love them," he would explain patiently. "And how do you do that? Send that love right down the hoe handle and give the pig a pat on the head every day."

He then cautioned: "Of course, it is here where you

must be extremely careful. You must never, ever give the pig any indication that some day he or she would be served up with a big bowl of sauerkraut.

They get wind of that," he said, "and you'll not only end up with a skinny pig, but a cantankerous one as well. I made that mistake just once and I learned my lesson. There was no keeping him penned up and a meaner pig never lived. Why, mother had to do her washings at night while the critter slept. Otherwise, her entire wash found its way ground into the dirt."

Pearly stopped and thought a moment. "Fact is," he said, "the dang bugger even got wind of her doing that and would stay awake just waiting for her to fill the clothesline. Even putting the clothesline on the porch did no good."

Pearly's wife then resorted to hanging the laundry all over the house, including in the cellar. "To put an end to this pig's rowdiness is to compare it to an unruly child. You know how some spoiled brats balk when they don't get their way? You know, like when they refuse to eat or go to the bathroom properly. Well, pigs can be just like that only even more so, especially if they get the idea they may not continue to live the sheltered life they are accustomed to."

With Pearly's lesson with pigs over, he then switched the topic to raising turkeys. "I shoulda raised turkeys anyway," he told me that afternoon on the porch. "Those critters don't even have enough sense to come out of the rain. Why, you can chop a turkey's heads off right in front of all the rest and they think the guy was just getting a haircut.

"As for all the dancin' and floppin' around after the fool thing has been beheaded, I'm not sure what they think of those carrins' on," he said.

"Anyway, knowing turkeys as I do," he continued, "they probably think the old boy is just happy and showing his delight for being picked as the one to have his hair done."

As always with Pearly, the afternoon was a pleasant

one. Homemade lemonade and his famous date- and raisin-filled cookies filled our bellies. And once again I learned how Pearly would straighten this country out if he were president.

It's too bad some of his ideas can't be used in Augusta and Washington, actually. Especially the ones where he'd make certain that all the "dead wood" was floated down the Kennebec or Potomac and out to sea.

Although this is the Pearly most everyone knew, or thought they knew, there was another part of the man that was known only to his closest friends. I happened to be one of those friends and I've cherished that friendship all my life. It is this next account of Pearly's lifestyle that made him a true character.

First, it must be understood Pearly was not a wealthy man when it came to money. Oh, he worked every day at his job, but his wages were modest, since they came from woodworking factories in Maine. In addition, the income from his apple crop and cider mill probably did little more than pay his taxes each year.

Still the man had a wealth of wisdom, probably more than a dozen men combined. He had many so-called sayings that were really some of that individual wisdom. One of those "sayings" went something like this: *"To be really happy in life one must give to others even when he has nothing to give."*

So, this sets the stage for the "other" Pearly.

Every Christmas Eve this otherwise slim, tall and gangling man who wouldn't weigh 160 pounds wet takes his slightly hunched over body and transforms it into a perfectly shaped roly-poly Santa Claus. Why, even his facial appearances take on a totally different look.

His grayish beard and hair become snow white and his bony jowls blossom out like those of his pet sow. After he's donned the red suit he wears each December, Pearly takes on the look of a man who would easily tip the scales at 250 pounds or more.

How he makes this perfect transformation no one really knows. A Hollywood makeup artist would be hard-pressed to do a better job.

But, the perfect and most exact replica of St. Nick is his uncanny ability to know and understand his friends and neighbors. Somehow he seems to know, or at least have knowledge of, those families that will not be able to have the Christmas they want because of the lack of money for special holiday food, presents and decorations. Pearly makes certain that the deprived children are taken care of first. Still, there are a few of the adults in his midst who would go without at Christmas as well if it were not for Pearly's generosity and big heart.

How he does it on his own modest income no one really knows. This has been a mystery for the many, many years Pearly has been doing this. Those like myself do not question his motives, sincerity or, above all, where the money comes from for him to be so generous to those who have even less than he does.

The few close friends who know about Pearly's good and generous deeds each Christmas just accept it as a miracle. After all, didn't the true meaning and reason for Christmas begin nearly 2000 years ago with a miracle?

Whenever we mention Pearly as a character, we always put the adjective "wonderful" in front of it.

Chapter 5

The Untold Mystery of Silvo Packard

It would probably not surprise anyone that Silvo Packard's neighbors always called him "Silver." He was an enterprising fellow and, in spite of never working a full-time job, no one could ever describe him as lazy. He earned his keep, regardless of the season. He always seemed to eat regularly and somehow kept from freezing to death in the winter. So, one might ask, how did Silver manage to stay alive without being gainfully employed?

For one thing, Silver lived off the land. In other words, Mother Nature did a darned good job of looking after him. That's not to say he didn't give Mother Nature a hand from time to time. In fact, it was these skills that sustained him through the long Maine winter months.

Some say Silver was part Mohawk Indian and that some of his survival skills were in his genes, as they say. Silver's ability to barter for the things he needed and come out on top of the deal in most cases was remarkable. The gun he used to get most of the game he needed for food and clothing was an old 38/55 rifle that he traded with a local farmer for doing odd jobs around his farm.

This same farmer also provided Silver with a lot of hand-me-down clothing and footwear. Although some of the hand-me-downs were a bit too good for Silver to feel comfortable wearing, he never wasted a piece. Silver simply traded the apparel for something else he needed and could use more.

One could probably guess that Silver was always trying to stay ahead of the law, especially with the enactment of the new, modern game laws and the abundance of game wardens to enforce them.

I mean, when someone is accustomed to catching 15 trout or shooting an extra deer or two, it's mighty hard to change their ways. This was especially true when it came to the fish limit. A five-fish limit just never seemed to "cut it" for a meal when Silver was used to eating a plate of 15.

Of course, Silver was never choosy when it came to hunting big game. If a moose or doe happened into his sights while deer hunting, he wasn't at all hesitant about taking either—or both—of the critters. Besides, Silver always maintained the skins off does and moose tanned better for gloves and shoes than those off a rangy old buck. How much truth there was to this I don't think anyone knew! Anyway, it made for a good excuse for Silver's law breaking.

I do know Silver never thought much of the new bucks-only law being talked about in Augusta, the state capital. Perhaps all of the changes being enacted and talked about were just part of his natural defiance. If that were the case, it is certainly understandable especially if you happen to be part Native American.

To my knowledge, Silver never adhered to any of the new laws, especially if they were in conflict with his heritage and lifestyle. And, for the most part, most folks left Silver well enough alone. I guess they figured that here's a guy doing no harm to anyone, and making it on his own, so why stir the pot?

Another way Silver provided for himself was to fiddle at the Saturday night dances. Some of us even thought this fellow had the fiddling talent to make it big if he was a-mind to. Even at a dance Silver would barter for a plate of sandwiches and a piece of homemade cake rather than take all his cash payment for his fiddlin' services.

It was here where some of the mysteries of Silvo Packard emerged. First, where did the fiddle come from, or perhaps more importantly, how in the world did he ever learn to play it with such skill and perfection?

No one really knew where he picked up his fiddlin' talent; we just knew he was darned good at it. Silver could get the dancers really hopping with the knee-slapping tune "Turkey in the Straw" or turn the mood completely with the likes of "The Missouri Waltz."

There was certainly more good that could be said of the man than there was bad, in spite of his habit of breaking hunting and fishing laws.

His ability to concoct herbal medicines from plants and other vegetation in the forest was unique only to those of Native American heritage. The same could be said of Silver's woodcarving skills; birds, ducks and geese, as well as small animals, were his specialties.

These items were also a major commodity used in his bartering process. A favorite of the ladies were his driftwood dried wildflower centerpieces. These items alone provided many meals and an array of baked goods.

Most knew little about the history of Silver and those who did never knew his exact roots or where he came from. It was as though one day he appeared out of nowhere. Most knew he had taken up residence in an old abandoned sap house once used by a local farmer. He had bartered this humble shelter and firewood for work mending fences and doing other repairs around the farm.

His frequent trips into town were routed mostly through the woods. It was only when he reached the outskirts of town that he would emerge from the trees and use a main road. Some say he had a fear of automobiles, while others maintained that he would rather walk than ride.

Regardless, no one ever knew of him accepting a ride under any circumstance. All of these individual traits remained a mystery.

Although an entire book could be written about Silver, probably the most notable quality people admired about him was his positive outlook on life. No one ever heard him criticize anyone or anything. If he didn't agree with someone, or a particular issue, he minded his own business without uttering a word and therefore allowing the other person's argument or point of view to win the day.

Despite his isolation, if anyone needed a helping hand he always showed up to help, without any conditions except those presented by the person who needed help. Sometimes he'd accept those conditions and sometimes he would not. It all depended on the circumstance and whether those conditions were putting a burden on anyone. Whatever the outcome, the helping hand was always extended till the job was done.

It was only then that Silver would leave as silently as he had arrived, often before he could be thanked for his good deed.

Yes, Silver was a man most any town would be proud to count as a resident. But unfortunately, just as he would arrive one day, he could be gone the next. No one knew when or where he went. They only knew that for a while there was one man who had enriched all of their lives, void of all material things, but was still able to leave them with priceless memories.

The moral of the mystery is this: If you're ever lucky enough to run into someone like Silvo Packard in your travels, respect and learn from him. He'll make both you and your life much better for it.

And if you're *really* lucky, he might just offer you a nice venison dinner.

Chapter 6

The Wisdom of an Unnamed Character

As one can probably imagine, some characters choose not to be identified. Yet, they still have timeless stories to tell and wisdom to share.

This is one of those stories:

"Being of modest means," the storyteller began, "I've always wondered what it would feel like to be a famous person such as a movie star or well-known writer, or a combination of both, complete with lots and lots of wealth.

"Then again," he continued, "being a famous athlete like Ted Williams or a famous explorer such as Admiral Byrd might be nice. Well, I don't have to wonder any longer and this is what my story is about."

You see, a while back the storyteller had the good fortune of meeting a very wise man. No, he wasn't well-to-do or famous—or even well-known. Nevertheless, he was rich with God-given wisdom and he had the uncanny ability to put things in their proper perspective by using a great wealth of common sense. It was this man who set the storyteller straight about how it must feel to be someone else of great wealth or status.

"We are all put on this earth as human beings and if blessed with good health and fortune, we are able to

34

think and care for ourselves," he said.

"Secondly, we must go through a period of being a baby and on into adolescence and finally adulthood. During all of these phases of life, we experience the ways of the world. We are usually educated to some degree, whether it be at home, or at public or private schools. Some may even be more fortunate and go on to college. In addition, most probably we will receive some form of religious training or experience, unless you are a non-believer."

He continued: "Still, we must not overlook the fact that whether or not we believe in a higher power, or God, it will take exposure to the world to arrive at any given status."

The wise man told the storyteller that the ways of the world are much like traveling a prepared roadmap. "There will be many journeys that must be taken," he said. "Some will be on roads such as turnpikes and expressways, others on smooth two-lane highways, others on gravel, and still others on the bumpy dirty back roads that seem so plentiful in Maine and that are sometimes downright impassable.

"It goes without saying that the bumpy graveled and sometimes un-maintained roads will be the most difficult to negotiate, the wise man said.

"Regardless, at one time or another, we'll find ourselves on one of these roads in spite of our best efforts to avoid them," he said.

"Then there are our emotions," the wise man said,

adding that, "there would be happy times, sad times, glad times, and disappointing times throughout our life. We'll experience them all," he said.

"Some of us will have families, large and small. But whatever the size, there will be joyous times as well as sorrowful times. There will be births, but there will also be deaths. There will be successes and there will be failures.

"For all, there will be laughter, then again there will be tears," he continued. "Some will travel easier than others and some may have to walk the entire distance. Then there are others who may have to crawl.

"But fortunately, those who must walk or crawl may find a ride now and then with another person more fortunate," he said. "And you'll notice it is those who have the toughest times that often make the better human being.

"Finally, there are those whose transportation may fail them and they might not know how to walk, since they have never had to before, he said. "It is they who will have the toughest time of all on this journey through of life.

"So you see, things are all relative when put in the proper prospective," the wise man said. "If you ever want to know how the wealthy or famous feel, the answer is simple: They feel just the same as you or I. No better, no worse. It all depends upon many circumstances and the roads they have traveled."

When the wise man had finished, I could not resist

repeating the old adage that "everyone puts their pants on the same way—one leg at a time."

The wise man responded, "Not always. They might have to sit down, especially if they have trouble balancing on one leg!"

Chapter 7

Changing Times

Although my memories mainly focus on the characters I have met throughout my life, I also have a compelling interest in self-education, philosophy, politics and politicians and, perhaps above all, have become somewhat of a character myself.

For instance, in talking with a friend of mine the other day, he mentioned how he was having a hard time accepting the many changes that have taken place in his lifetime. I should mention this friend is a few years younger than I am. My response to him was, *"Welcome to the Club!"*

Then I said, "Hold on a minute. Let's put this monumental subject matter in its proper prospective."

"What do you mean?" he asked.

"Well hear me out for a few moments," I replied.

"Let's suppose you were born in the year 1850 and lived to the age of, say, 65, which of course is doin' pretty darned good back then. Now, in your lifetime you would have seen, or at least learned of slavery and the end of it. You have to admit that was a good thing.

"But let's continue on as we've only scratched the surface here," I continued. "You would have witnessed the coming of such things as the automobile, airplane and advances in communication such as the telegraph and telephone. But back then there were those who also had problems associated with all the advancements, just as we have problems with the advancements of today.

"Had you lived in that time period you might, and probably would have been, one of those people who struggled with the major changes to our country and way of life," I opined.

"For some back then, the trusted horse, or horse and buggy was just fine to get from one place to another. The danged automobile was just a miserable smelly nuisance to some, and moreover it was threatening their way of life. Many, and probably you included, would probably have said, 'Why couldn't some folk just leave well enough alone? So what if there are some who don't like horses, they don't need to spoil it for the rest of those who do.'"

"And as far as the telephone goes," he asked, "what more long distance communication was needed? My friend and many other people did just fine with the telegraph. It had served their needs well.

"Remember, it only took three days for your sister Harriet in Boston to learn of your first-born," I said. "Besides who wants all those confounded wires strung all over kingdom-come anyway?

"Of course, Darwin was messing around with evolution in your early days," I reminded him, "but his work would be no threat to your lifestyle or religious beliefs. Nevertheless, you did not approve of his work. You might have been "right on" with that one though," I said.

I was getting warmed up. "The invention of the mowing machine was already on board by the time that you bought your first farm. It was still a bit of work keeping the thing operational, as breakdowns were frequent. It seemed, too, the confounded cutter blade was always dull and needed sharpening.

"You were some glad though to see Mr. Gillette make his appearance and bring about the new safety razor. Still you maintained it could never replace your trusted straight razor. 'Too hard to keep the dang thing from clogging up with whiskers,' you said, especially when you were in a hurry.

"Still there were things coming down the road that drove you nearly insane and you were convinced they would put you in the poor house," I said.

"Electricity had advanced and brought about many of the goodies that run on the darned stuff. There was the coming of the vacuum cleaner, toaster, washing machine and other items that made your wife Edna's life a lot easier.

"There was one thing you did welcome, though, and it was the electric welder. Although it wasn't perfected yet and needed a bit of expertise to operate, the invention saved you a lot of time with some of your machinery breakdowns."

My friend continued listening; I continued talking.

"Another thing that you were really grateful for was the coming about of local anesthesia. You had just about enough of that ether drip that made you sicker'n a dog in a pile of chicken bones when you had your first farm mishap. And thank goodness for the x-ray machine; they may never have discovered that break in your wrist without it."

I told my friend that social issues were not high on his list of pet peeves, but many others concerning the male population were indeed of interest to him. Although women had not yet gained the right to vote in his lifetime, he felt threatened by the Women's Suffrage Movement. He and Edna were on opposite sides of the fence on this issue.

"Probably a good thing though," I told him, "since you were able to maintain a decent weight from spending many nights in the barn without your supper."

Chapter 8

The Great Depression of 1929

My recollection of The Great Depression is virtually non-existent except for the accounts passed down by my parents, grandparents and others, as well as newspaper articles that they had saved.

If my math is correct, my parents would have been in their early 20s and my grandparents in their late 40s during the dark, hardscrabble years of the Depression, which was triggered by the unprecedented stock market crash of 1929.

For it was this date, October 29, 1929, when those trading in the stock market panicked, provoking a massive sell-off. The crash meant financial ruin for many, as mills and factories closed their doors and several banks failed. Overnight, millions of people lost their jobs. Many of them would then lose their homes, farms and small businesses.

It was a time when Americans pulled together in a way the country had never before experienced. Unfortunately, there were some people who could not withstand the terrible burden and they resorted to suicide. Those who had the will and fortitude survived in many ways. In my family, for instance, many of the children of my grandparents would return to their families to live—back to their nests, so to speak, to seek refuge from the elements and find food for themselves and their children.

Every member of the family contributed any way they could. The men folk took work of any kind, part-time if necessary, as laborers or anything else that might bring in a few pennies or dollars. The women took in washings from those better off than they, to earn whatever money they could.

Fortunately, my grandparents lived on a small farm where all of their children had been raised. They continued to grow and can as many of the vegetables as they could. Still, with an addition of 14 or more mouths to feed, food rationing was a must. Salt pork, salt pork gravy and corn meal mush became a frequent meal. Soups made from ham or beef bones also were high on the menu, as were baked beans and a variety of hashes.

Those less fortunate resorted to the nearest bread lines, as very few were being spared the dire poverty that most of the country was forced to deal with daily.

This also must have been the first great rush of what we now call "today's homeless". Then, according to my grandparents, they were called tramps or hobos, but as I understand it, they were never called bums.

Many found shelter in train boxcars, or anywhere else that provided shelter from the elements. Although some people were badly in need of baths, as well as other elements of personal hygiene, it is also my understanding that they, regardless of their condition, were never refused food or an item of clothing that was badly needed.

Of course, charity was dependent on whether there was food and items of clothing to give. Many went away both hungry and cold. Cardboard in the soles of shoes and other footwear was always used to get more wear out of them and regardless of their condition, they were never discarded.

Social status had very little meaning since those who were once wealthy now joined the ranks of the poor. Eventually, federal government work programs emerged. Two in particular that were mentioned by my grandparents and my parents were the Civilian Conservation Corps and the Work Projects Administration. I'm told even the most sophisticated and previously well-to-do citizens had no problem standing shoulder-to-shoulder with the less fortunate.

There are many stories that would stagger the imagination of the hardships so many endured during these long, hard years. Yet, I'm told that those who survived became better men and women because or in spite of it. I often wonder what it would take to shock some of us into becoming a better people today.

Those of us who have never experienced, first hand, the depression of 1929 cannot know how we would we react, how would we cope—even more importantly, how we would handle such financial disaster.

Could you possibly imagine having to live without the luxuries we enjoy today? What about if our kids and grandkids were deprived of their material items? Talk about hysteria.

Well there is probably one thing for certain: the homeless now among us would get along just fine, as would those who do not put much stock in material wealth. But for others there might be a problem.

As for myself, I'm glad I know what it's like to wear cardboard in the bottom of my shoes to get a few more weeks of wear out of them.

Even a diet of salt pork, salt pork gravy and corn meal mush could be tolerated. In fact it might be a welcome change.

But having the entire family come back to roost? . . . I would have to think long and hard about that one.

Chapter 9

More About Changes

While on the subject of changes, I remember well what my childhood was like at Thanksgiving and Christmas. It would seem that this account of Thanksgiving, although it took place many years ago, still might be of interest to many.

As a youngster, all I remember being purchased at the stores and the up-and-coming supermarkets were a few items my father couldn't grow and my mother and grandmother couldn't make. This was not only the case on a daily or weekly basis, but especially true at Thanksgiving and at Christmas time.

Can anyone today possibly imagine feeding and preparing everything for Thanksgiving and Christmas and purchasing less than a couple dozen items for both events? We are talking about providing everything for nine people in the case of my family—four grown ups and five children. This would include all food and the items for gifts and presents.

If my memory serves me correctly, the only items I recall coming from the stores were fresh cranberries, nuts still in their shells, spices, yeast, flour, and sugar for mother's homemade bread and rolls, pies, cookies and cakes. Also, I remember the olive and celery dish served during the holidays, so I have to believe those items, too, were purchased. One thing for certain, though, the variety of pickles, pickled beets, and relish, set out beautifully on a tray, were all products from my grandmother's and grandfather's root cellar and our own hand-dug cellar at our house.

The bird, usually a prize Tom or rooster, was killed and dressed the day before, and then stuffed with homemade bread crumbs and other basic ingredients. All vegetables were grown from our garden, along with the apples we picked up at a nearby orchard. Even the ingredients—except for the spices—used for squash and pumpkin and the custard and mincemeat pies were all home-prepared.

Fresh milk was delivered every day or two in quart glass bottles that used to support more than six inches of cream on top. In cold winter mornings, this head of cream would push the cardboard cap from the bottle and then find its way out into the outside air much like a vertical frozen stalagmite.

Fresh eggs from our own hens served as the basic ingredient for mother's delicious custard and other pies. Cookies and cakes were all made from recipes that called for many other store-bought items such as raisins, dates, currents and figs.

I suppose coconut was also purchased from the store, but it was a whole coconut in the shell which had to be cracked open and the coconut meat removed.

In addition there were fresh fruits such as lemons, oranges, bananas, and possibly grapes, although we did have purple grape vines in our midst that were there for the picking.

I also imagine toiletries such as soap and toilet paper were purchased, although I seem to remember the possibility of lye soap being made at home. One thing for sure was that ketchup, root beer, horseradish, rhubarb for pies, and tomato juice were all prepared at our home. Even a tray of homemade hog's-head cheese was available at the pig-butchering time.

So what was a typical Thanksgiving dinner like? Probably much the same as it is today, minus the many so-called "put-up" preserves or "made-from-scratch" pastries. For example, there were always the old standby squash or pumpkin pies, as well as apple, of course.

However, "goodies" such as date- or raisin-filled cookies, banana-cream pie, homemade mince-meat pie, and a variety of puddings were topped with a hardsauce. Then there were always cream puffs with a homemade filling and the unfairly-maligned fruitcake, along with tarts filled with a generous amount of handpicked wild strawberry jam.

Could anyone who lived during that time possibly forget the "made from scratch" stuffing with pieces of ground up liver, gizzards, and heart from the bird that sat in the middle of the dinner table? But perhaps most unforgettable of all was a generous helping of homemade grape-nut ice cream that sometimes followed dinner.

Yes, those were hard times—at least harder than today. But neither I, nor many of my friends, would change a thing.

Today, Thanksgiving and other family times are not just consumed by preparing, cooking and eating a feast. After over-stuffing ourselves on turkey and all the trimmings at my sister's home one holiday, the grandchildren disappeared into a room to play games, only they were on computers, a TV, or small pocket-sized electronic devices.

"Remember Dick," my sister said, "we did the same thing back 65 years ago, only the games were a bag of marbles and a handful of jacks."

One parent who overheard our conversation, quipped, "I bet those didn't cost 500 dollars, either!"

Chapter 10

The Chainin' Gang

I have been blessed to have a close friend who owns a camp on the northern shore of Moosehead Lake. Perhaps it will be difficult for some to understand, especially those who have never had the chance to visit one of Maine's most beautiful and famed lakes, why it is such an absolute delight to visit there.

This is especially true when spending time with my friend at his camp on Moosehead, both during the heat of summer and the frigid cold of winter. In winter, along with ice-fishing, comes an abundance of snowmobile touring over the hundreds of miles of tote and logging roads covered by a canopy of snow-laden trees.

However, during one particular winter, I was introduced to an entirely different form of winter fun; at least that is what the inventor of this new activity called it. The inventor of this new event just happened to be my friend's camp neighbor and for purposes of this story we'll just call him Don. Now, my friend has had his camp since the very late 1960s and early 1970s and his neighbor-friend Don arrived through a sale of the neighboring camp in the mid-1980s. Although I had briefly met Don a few times before what would become known later as an escapade, I never really knew him well.

However, by the time this escapade was over Don had earned the title of "character."

This new invention I'm talking about is called "chainin'!" This hobby of chainin' is one heck of a lot of work, and much like most hobbies, it entails collecting. Of course, whether or not it is a lot of work depends upon one's point of view. To the collector, especially Don, it was all fun and games. In fact, for this camp neighbor it happened to be a thrill of a lifetime.

There are no rules or guidelines for this hobby of chainin'. In fact, it's every man for himself, and backbiting, backstabbing, and even stealing is considered acceptable and it is all part of the game or "hobby."

Oh, there may be the usual grumbling and even some cuss words of "unfair play" from other collectors, but the loser must just consider himself outwitted. To do anything other than lick one's wounds, and ride off into the sunset, so to speak, would just be considered being a poor sport.

As previously stated, chainin' is collecting. But not just any chains, mind you, but those chains that are specifically called, and were used as, "boom chains".

For the younger readers who might not know, boom chains were usually handcrafted in blacksmith shops during the 18th and early 19th centuries. They were used to connect the massive timbers, called booms, together to help control the floating of logs or pulpwood down a body of water. In other words, these so-called booms helped keep the wood from dispersing as it made its way down rivers or lakes—a common practice in Maine until the Clean Water Act of the 1960s, ironically, perhaps, authored and championed by Maine U.S. Senator Edmund Muskie.

To give some idea of the size of these booms and chains that held them together is to say a boom might be as much as eighty feet in length with a diameter of two to three feet, and the chain that secured them together, as much as an inch in diameter by twelve to twenty feet in length and would weigh up to sixty or more pounds per chain.

With that description, can anyone possibly imagine why any person would want to collect them? They are so darn big and heavy you couldn't pull anything with them. Why it's doubtful if anyone other than Hulk Hogan could even get one hooked to a stuck car or pickup. Even if a person was lucky enough to get one hooked up, the "puller-outer" probably wouldn't have strength enough to even take the slack out of the darn thing.

And after you get chains, what are you going to do with them? Hang them on the wall next to a portrait of grandpa or your favorite wedding picture—I don't think so! Not only would it probably pull the sheetrock clean off the wall, the wife would have you sleeping in the spare room for a month or more. Surely you wouldn't have one stuffed in your hip pocket so every time you met a friend or distant relative you could pull it out and say, "Hey, look at my new hobby. I'm now a collector of boom chains!"

Still, I understand Don has some innovative ideas for his keepsakes. He is constructing a 360-degree pole-fence around his camp and he plans to drape these "beauties" all along this fence. In fact, I'm told he already has the project underway and a few chains are also already on display. Trouble is, he has encountered an unexpected problem: it seems the top rail that is supporting most of the weight has taken the shape of a sway-backed horse.

Let's get on with my adventure of collecting these treasures.

When the log-drives ceased years back, many of the chains were either disconnected from the boom logs by humans and used for other purposes such as bridge and wharf construction or dimension lumber or came unhooked from their booms or timbers by rot or just plain rough water and sank to the bottom or remained on the shores of rivers and lakes. However, there are many chains that still remain connected to the booms that floated up on the shores of some lakes. One of these lakes was Seboomook Lake just a few miles northwest of Moosehead Lake. This would be where our assault would take place, up and down the shores of Seboomook Lake.

Seboomook is several miles long. Like many man-made lakes in the winter, it suffers from lack of water. Certainly bad news for many wild species such fish, ducks and geese or other water-living mammals, but it makes for ideal conditions for chainin'.

Anyway, this venture started at the most northern end of Moosehead Lake in the wee hours of the morning on snowmobiles each pulling a dog sled. It's important to understand that I had no idea what I was in for, or where I was going. All I knew for sure was that it was colder than the Artic Circle and my hands and feet were probably going to be a block of ice before this adventure was over.

As we passed the Seboomook Camp Grounds, our first landmark before reaching our designated location more than ten miles away on the north shore of Seboomook, Don stopped to reassure us that, "This is going to be a thrill of a lifetime."

With that prediction, we all put the hammer down and in a short while we reached our first destination. I could only assume this was our first stop on our trip because up ahead the lead rider and prime chain collector had already stopped his machine, dismounted and had his hands waving in the air like he had just made a winning touchdown at the Super Bowl. Finally, with all machines shut off, we also realized Don was also shouting at the top of his lungs "Here they are; here are my little jewels." As it turned out, his "jewels" were a bunch of ugly looking old rusty chains draped over a number of stumps.

At the time I never gave it a thought as to how Don knew exactly where these chains were located, much less the circumstances of how they were all conveniently assembled in one place. It turned out that this friend of Don's came upon these chains during the last deer season and spent nearly the entire day digging them out of the sandy shoreline and other places, then assembled them on stumps so he could pick them up during the upcoming snowmobile season. In any event, Don somehow found out his friend's discovery and secret location, and, unbeknown to me, I was about to be involved in a theft greater than the Brinks Bank robbery of years past.

With snow so deep it nearly reached our crotches, we struggled for more than two hours to get all the chains loaded onto our dog sleds. It was then it finally came to me and I suddenly realized that I was now chainin' and I had just (allegedly) experienced "the thrill of a lifetime!"

What I couldn't understand was why I wasn't jumping for joy with excitement like this other guy Don, who couldn't have been happier if he had just found a gold mine. Seriously, I had to figure this guy must own everything else in the world and the acquisition of these ugly things (chains) would finally put him on top of the heap.

With our dog sleds finally loaded with more chains than I could count, we were again underway and headed for the next location. Another half hour took us across the lake and onto the opposite shore, where this time there were no chains draped over the exposed stumps.

"Why are we stopping here?" my friend quizzed Don.

"Have patience," Don replied, "they are here. I can feel them in the air!

"Feel what?" I asked as all I felt was the bitter cold which had already penetrated my boots, nearly freezing my toes.

"Chains!" Don yelled. "They are here and all we have to do is find them. See that monstrous tree over there with all the roots exposed? That's where my jewels are hiding," Don said.

As we moved our machines closer to the huge tree, sure enough a link or two of a chain appeared. "There they are, just as I predicted," Don hollered. He could see our doubt and confusion. "Look, I may have said this trip was going to be a thrill of a lifetime, but I never said it was going to be easy," he admonished. "Come on, get out your hatchets and start chopping away at that frozen ice and soil around them."

We were all hoping that Don was as good at chainin' as he was giving orders. Two hours had passed and our hatchet blades were worn to a frazzle, not to mention we were sweating like butchers, and we had uncovered a total of three chains. Fortunately for our collector, but perhaps unfortunately for the rest of us, we had exposed links of perhaps a dozen more chains.

"Okay," Don orders, "we need to change our game plan of retrieval; we'll build a fire and smoke 'em out."

Good gracious, I thought, *is there anything this guy won't do to get a boom chain?* Apparently not, since we then found ourselves lugging all the dried firewood we could muster from the nearby tree branches and other dried wood that lies loose on the shoreline.

We surrounded the exposed roots of that tree with more wood than a bonfire for a University of Maine football rally, then "touched her off" using bunches of gasoline soaked paper towels. In no time we had started an inferno that would make a pyromaniac quiver in his boots. And before long we had links of chain exposed everywhere. Honestly, it was like a giant octopus coming out of the ground. For the first time I was beginning to enjoy this chainin'—especially when Don got the idea to hook his snowmobile onto a link and yank the remainder of the chain free from its burial plot.

The snowmobile retrieval process worked wonders —to our delight and, I must admit, surprise. Before long, all dog sleds, running boards and rear carriers of our snowmobiles were draped with the "jewels" from the shores of Seboomook. With all snowmobile belts burned half off from all the weight of the loads, the ride back to our original destination was essentially uneventful. And I must admit it was "something" of a lifetime, whether or not it was a "thrill" . . . I've got to think a while longer on that one.

Chapter 11

Diapers, Duct Tape, and a Day with Grandpa

If you really want to have some fun, take a two-year-old grandson to camp with you for a few days. That was what a friend of mine told me the other day. He happens to be a friend who also has a camp in the north woods on Moosehead Lake.

It seems this friend's camp neighbor, (yup, the chainin' guy) made an unexpected visit to his camp a while back along with one of his friends and a two-year-old grandson. As the story goes, it was a bundle of laughs from the time they arrived until they left, which was only about three hours later.

I guess the one thing that made this episode so interesting—to say the least—was the absence of the young fellow's mother, father, or grandmother. In other words, these two guys were on their own with this little bundle of joy.

It is my understanding that although this little guy was being potty trained at home, a trip to the north is quite another matter. As one can probably imagine, the inevitable happened and, although they were smart enough to bring diapers along, they weren't all that proficient in installing one.

In fact when a change was required at my friend's camp, a wide band of gray duct tape—Maine's "official tool," as it's often called, made an appearance around the little guy's midsection.

"What in the world is this?" my friend quizzed of his camp neighbors.

The answer was relatively simple and it had a wee bit of Yankee ingenuity attached to the answer as well. "Darned diaper wouldn't stick or stay put on so we just dug out some trusted duct tape and by gorry as you can see, never had a problem after that."

As a common courtesy, my friend then lent a helping hand and demonstrated to his camp neighbors just how a store-bought diaper should be installed. This would be a first for his camp, so a note along with the time and date was recorded into his logbook.

With the little guy's personal hygiene taken care of my friend offered his two camp neighbors some refreshments and coffee, which they both accepted. By this time the little guy was making himself right at home by opening every cupboard he could reach and eating a dog bone he found behind the wood box. Then in just a fraction of a second, a mousetrap went off with an unforgettable snap, and at the same time there came a bloodcurdling yell that nearly dislodged the pots and pans from their shelves.

Before any of us could react, the little fella came running from the kitchen with his entire hand engulfed in the trap. With tears streaming down his cheeks and his hand shaking and waving like a flag in a hurricane trying to get the thing off, his grandfather was now in a cardiac-arrest panic. Luckily, my friend stayed calm, removed the beast that had attacked the toddler, and nursed circulation back into the hand that has already began to turn black and blue.

In no time at all, the little guy was back on the mend and exploring every nook and cranny in the camp. Just as things seemed to have quieted down and now under control, the little explorer (future Admiral Byrd) shows up with a partially opened and partially empty box of D-CON mouse poisoning.

The grandfather now slips into a real panic and goes completely berserk. While he was struggling with emotions to keep from having a heart attack, the other two men determine that the little Marco Polo hasn't eaten any of the poison.

Finally, with the grandfather breathing normal again, things began to settle down. The grandfather, now a nearly total nervous wreck, does not take his eye off this little bundle of fun for the remainder of his visit.

And since the friend didn't hear reports of any camps burning down or major forest fires, he assumed the little guy was back home safely and none for the worse.

Thank the Lord for small miracles!

Chapter 12

Humming Along—Not!

Remember the friend who has the camp in the North Woods on Moosehead Lake and remember his camp neighbors? If you ask, "Would that be the neighbor who brought his two-year-old grandson to camp with him and nearly disfigured the kid for life? Also the chainin' guy?

The answer would be: "Yup, that's the guy."

With this guy identified it's time to tell another one of his stories. Once again I was invited to my friend's camp and as luck would have it my friend's camp neighbor was there also. It seems once you get to know this neighbor he starts to fall into that category as a "character." That is to say this guy has some really strange ways to entertain himself.

We have already told the story relating to his hoarding of boom-chains. Still, there are other crazy things that qualify this guy to be considered a character. The guy is really one of the good guys once you get to know him and understand what makes him "tick." Also, because of years of hard work by both himself and his wife, they have been blessed with some of the finer things in life.

One of those items, which incidentally is somewhat

difficult not to be envious of, is an immaculate and well decked out "Hummer 2." I mean to say this is one beautiful machine that is absolutely equipped for any challenge the great North Woods might offer. That is, except for getting mired up to the running boards in a sinkhole during the spring thaw.

The story takes place on one of his favorite roads called S-2 and doing what he loves to do best next to chainin'—looking for moose horns. Moose often shed their horns along and just off this road, and next to collecting boom chains, finding moose horns comes in as a close second favorite hobby of my camp friend. In fact behind his camp wood stove looks like an extension to the State of Maine Museum: Moose horns are stacked from floor to ceiling.

Despite all the assurances from this character to his friend riding with him that the Hummer was immune to getting stuck, the inevitable happened. Probably the word "stuck" was an understatement as about three to five miles from the end of the so-called S-2 Road, this imitation of the great Hum Vee—a military version even—was now completely off the road and up to its doors in one of the great North Woods' spring sinkholes.

To make the story a little simpler to follow, let's once again call our character, Don and his passenger friend, Devroe.

As they came to an abrupt stop in this sinkhole, Don looks over to Devroe and says, "Not to worry. Just a push of this button here and we'll be in 4-wheel drive and back on to the main road before Rue (Don's dog) can give another yip."

With 4-wheel-drive engaged and mud flying off all 4 wheels more than 20 feet into the air, this beautiful machine sinks even deeper into this seemingly bottomless pit of Maine spring mud.

Now it's Devroe who looks over to Don and says, "Somethin' tells me with that mud flyin' in all directions and we haven't moved an inch, we is considered being stuck!"

Don fires back, "Impossible. You can't get one of these stuck. *It's a Hummer, remember?*"

"Now this may be a Hummer," Devroe retorts, "but from all indications and the fact that we haven't moved and with that mud being thrown nearly into the Seboomook Camp Grounds something tells me we're just about as stuck in this mud hole as that duct tape was to that little fella a while back!"

Don pried the door free and stepped out into the mud, which reached to his knees. Devroe heard him grumble, "You can't get a Hummer stuck."

Devroe then said, "Tell me, buddy, when you decide we might be stuck, I'll help to decide what we've got to do to get us out of this pickle."

With everything mired in mud and nothing showing but the body of the once-immaculate Hummer, Don was forced to face reality. "By gosh, it is possible to get a Hummer stuck!"

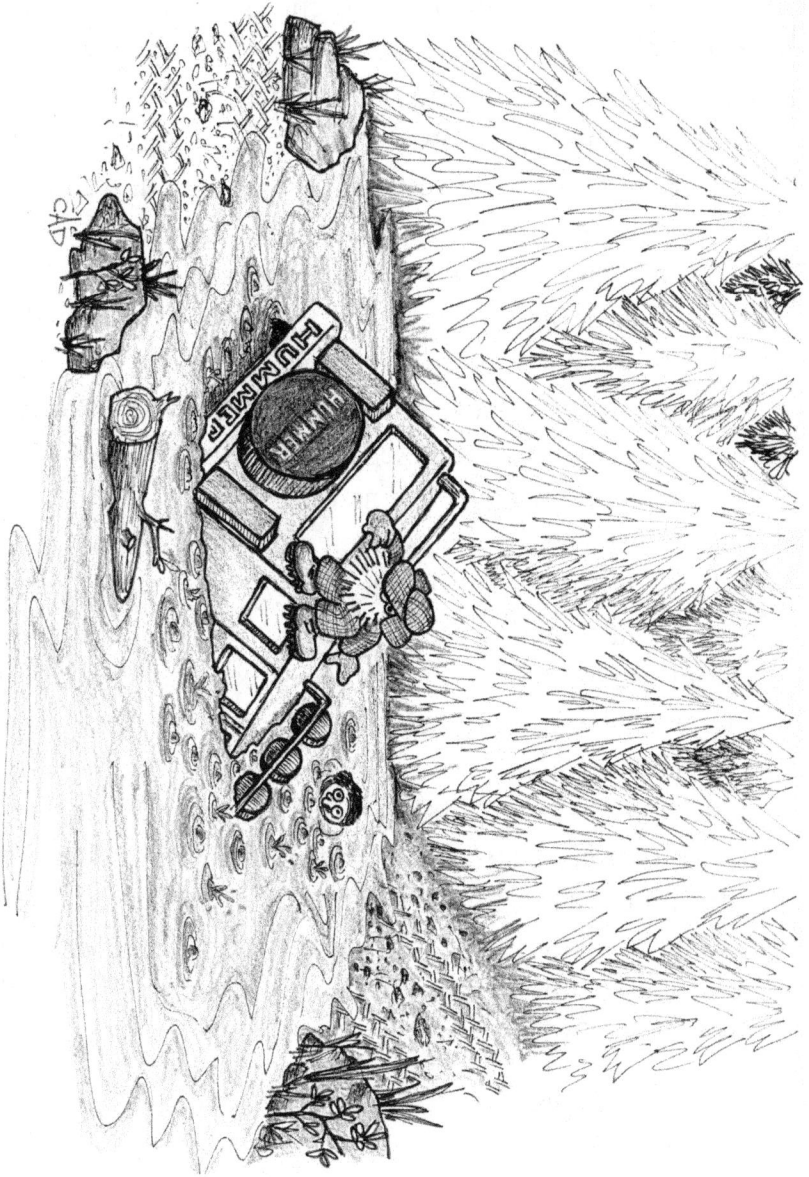

Six hours later, thanks to General Motors, its On-Star invention, and the trustworthy AAA road service, a wrecker had been called from nearly 100 miles away and the two men were once again back on the road.

When other friends told this story to Ed and Shirley Raymond, co-owners of Raymond's Country Store in Northeast Carry and two people who may be the final word in "happenings" in the North Woods, Ed was able to put the ordeal in its proper perspective.

He began, "Since the opening of these North Woods, there hasn't been a motorized contraption regardless of size that hasn't been stuck at one time or another. In fact, D-9 bulldozers have gotten stuck and it took other D-9 dozer, along with a skidder or two and an excavator, to get it out. So if anyone believes a Hummer can't get stuck up here in one of these sinkholes, especially during the spring thaw, well, let me just say this to put this issue to bed."

He concluded, "This fellow Don can thank his lucky stars that he still has a Hummer to drive. I would say, based on what I have been told of the incident, by all rights he should be holding a yearly memorial at that sinkhole where that Hummer would still be well on its way to China."

Chapter 13

Happy Campers

After three years as a widower, a friend of mine finally married a wonderful lady who also lost her husband to illness. They both had children and after about a year of marriage decided it was time for a vacation. Two of the children, both girls and teenagers, were the mothers' and the teenaged boys belonged to the father. It probably goes without saying this family may not have been the Brady Bunch, but for the most part they co-existed quite well.

They all mutually agreed to take a camping vacation, something that wasn't totally new to any of them. However, to say they were experienced campers would probably be an overstatement. With two vehicles packed like covered wagons, the venture began. It would be more than a 5-hour ride to their destination, so everyone was cautioned to take care of all their necessary bathroom duties before they left home.

Precisely six hours and fifty-five minutes later, and what seems like a dozen or more unscheduled "pit stops," they arrived at their campsite. As the story was told, it was here where the fun really started.

There would be four tents to assemble, one for the

two girls, another for the boys and a third for the mother and father. Another tent would be used as a utility and storage area for food and other miscellaneous camping essentials.

Although they had started before sun up, the chore was finished just barely before complete darkness enveloped their camp site. *What's going on here?* the father asked himself as he remembered the L.L. Bean salesperson assuring him that each tent, even with just one person at work, could be erected in a half-hour. Instead, with the help of two boys and two girls, they had been at it for more than six hours.

With the tents finally assembled and ready for occupancy, it was that time in the evening when the place swarms with visitors. Unfortunately, those visitors are black flies and mosquitoes. However, with the air painted blue with insect repellant, the unwelcome guests are kept somewhat under control.

Well, somehow everyone gets through the first day except for one of the boys who keeps getting the parents up because of a bellyache from eating too many M&M's with peanuts. After several doses of bellyache medicine, the site is quiet and everyone enjoys two whole hours of sleep that night.

The finale took place on the afternoon of the fourth day. An all-day canoe trip had been planned using only two canoes on a somewhat distant but popular canoeing river. Except for a few spills going down some of the shallow rips, the trip for the most part was enjoyable and uneventful. With everyone exhausted and hungry, they arrived back at their campsite looking forward to a meal that had been prepared ahead of time.

What they found was a visit from other unannounced guests, only these guests were one of the biggest thieves in the Maine woods. The footprints were easily identifiable and the claw marks on the coolers told them they had been visited by two very big—and hungry—black bears.

Tired and hungry themselves and with half the group scared to death, it was obvious there had to be a change of plans. Most notably was to pack up as quickly as possible and make tracks themselves.

Just how the remainder of the vacation was spent continues to be unclear. What was clear, though, was that the nearest motel and restaurant got some unexpected business that night. There also was a whole lot of camping gear for sale—cheap.

Chapter 14

Who's the Boss?

When a friend told me once that he planned to take on a person who loved and kept animals, I was hesitant to ever mention the subject matter to anyone again—especially to never write about it for all to read. I could imagine death threats coming from all across the state or from anywhere else that this story might wander. I certainly do not have the wisdom, know-how and knowledge that my friend has, so who am I to doubt his ideas on animals? Time will tell if he miscued on this one or not.

This story has nothing to do with being abusive to pets or animals or in anyway meant to harm domestic pets. In fact, it is really about giving pets their long-overdo credit for their relationships with humans. Credit which for too long humans have taken credit for and have claimed possession of. My friend believes from years of experience that "people do not train pets, pets train people." Now, hold up all you folks on your way to the closet or gun cabinet to load up 'Ole Betsy to blow this writer's head off. Hear me out, first.

Remember my friend, Pearly, the old farmer who recognized how pigs knew if they were being raised for their benefit or his. Well, Pearly also had Beagle dogs. We all know Beagles are great hunting dogs, especially when chasing rabbits. We also know for the most part they instinctively just love to hunt. Well for years Pearly has bragged endlessly to anyone who would listen just how well he trained his pet Beagles to run and hunt rabbits.

Well, here's the real truth: Pearly had absolutely nothing to do with those dogs running or hunting rabbits. The truth is those dogs love to hunt and they have learned that the best way for them to hunt is to drive the rabbits across Pearly's path so he could have them for his next night's supper. Besides, the Beagles were always well rewarded with treats and Pearly's "show off" affection each time he successfully bagged one of the wild critters.

Still not convinced who trained whom here? Let's take another look.

If you've ever been to the Pittston Farm in the North Woods, you know Ken, the owner, is an animal-lover. Ken has two parrots, one named Pretty Girl, and the other … well I can't remember, but I'm not sure it makes a lot of difference for the story.

Perhaps, too, I am mistaken by calling his little darlings, "parrots" when it actually may be that they're Macaws—still a parrot breed. For purposes of this story, their true breed doesn't really matter as they, too, have learned how to train humans. Especially Ken.

If you know anything at all about Macaw parrots, they tend to be somewhat of a show-off. These guys and gals are no exception. To get human attention, which is most always followed by treats (like Pearly's Beagles), they squawk so loud they can be heard half way to Millinocket. No small feat for birds with such small feet. When they hanker for a treat or attention, they just begin with this blood curdling scream, which is nearly deafening, by the way, until Ken or his guest showed up to nurse and fulfill their addictions.

Once again, who has trained whom here?

I have another friend who thinks he's the greatest thing to pets since the New York Dog Show.—Now there's a spectacle for you!— He carries a bag of dog bones everywhere he goes. In his daily travels, he has a few favorite dogs that he patronizes with his assortment of bones. Just because one or two of them will speak or roll over when he makes an appearance or offers his bones, my friend thinks he's the greatest animal trainer in the world. The guy has no idea that without his bag of bones he'd just be another jerk human invading their territory. In fact, they wouldn't give him a second sniff (no pun intended). I think the dogs would probably tell him to, "woof it out his ear."

As mentioned earlier, the best example of animal training is the New York Dog Show. As an animal-lover myself, I really don't like the show. Here we have dogs from every breed and nation in the world that prance around like they are the only living creatures on the planet. But the truth is, these animals are bathed, shampooed, and curry-combed into near ecstasy by their owners or handlers. They travel first class and are put up in fancy hotels that you or I could never hope to afford. They are given royal treatment only afforded to kings and some well-to-do politicians we all know

My friend says, "Is it any wonder these little darlings perform a few tricks, jump though hoops, and obey every command from their owners? Who wouldn't do the same if showered with that kind of treatment? Why even a husband has learned how to get along in ecstasy with his beloved wife: just let her believe she has *you* trained just like she does her animals!"

Chapter 15

Halloween Pranks from the Past

The older folks reading these stories might remember how Halloween pranks were commonplace when we were kids. Halloween night was not only unsupervised for anyone over five years old, but was especially a source of fun for the average teenager.

Now, Halloween is pretty much just treats handed out at a highly supervised "trick or treat" party at someone's house or in the school gym. Even with that protection, bags of candy must be well inspected. Yup, the "trick" has been taken out of Halloween in most neighborhoods.

But years ago, for the so-called "really good kids," many local churches opened their basement areas for all sorts of fun and games, refreshments of cider and doughnuts, a variety of sandwiches and popcorn balls held together with a mixture of caramel and molasses.

But there was another group of youngsters who created their own fun and entertainment on the bewitching holiday. These were not really "bad" kids, like some of today's young delinquents. To the contrary, they were just a bunch of kids who were, shall we say, a little more … creative … at having fun after dark on Halloween.

I must admit to being part of those fun-loving pranksters who caused harmless, yet obvious, trouble: the famous morning-after scene of toilet paper strung around trees like crooked garland around a Christmas fir. Rolls upon rolls were thrown up to the highest branches of what seemed every tree in town. As the loose paper from the roll caught a branch the remainder of the roll would uncoil, leaving a tail of white clear to the ground. The roll was then picked up and readied for it next journey to the top of the next tree. I am not sure why, but this prank was almost always carried out by boys. There was something comical about it to us. We had a blast, until the light of day exposed our misdeeds.

Some Octobers, the paper seemed to mingle in harmony with an early snow.

We were the pioneers in what is known today as "civil disobedience." Of course, I suppose our actions back then were the equivalent of what committing a robbery is today. The difference being that we had no real statements to make nor did we harm anyone but ourselves. We were just getting our "licks" in, so to speak, without doing any real damage. In truth, I must admit that some of us were getting back at the Strong selectmen for barring us the right to ride our bicycles atop the bridge over the Sandy River on the outskirts of town.

Yes, to ride across a two-foot-wide beam 60 feet over the river would seem even dumber than tossing toilet paper. But it was more fun than dumb.

Perhaps our greatest achievement in Halloween pranks was foiled when our plans went haywire one holiday. On this particular Halloween night, we had borrowed a hay wagon—more often called a hayrack back then—from our farmer friend, Charlie. You remember Charlie the farmer with the two-toned Model-A? Well, Charlie is not much for putting his equipment away and his hayrack was sitting out in his field just a few feet from the road.

We couldn't resist. We later would wish we would have.

We were all delighted when we arrived at the site where our genius prank was to be carried out. There

was going to be no problem getting the hayrack to the road and hooked onto the Model-A pickup owned by my friend Smithy's parents. The problem was going to be getting it the three miles up (what is now) Route 4 and into Strong without being caught.

Strong village back then was a section of Main Street about the length of a football field. It hosted stores on one side and a post office, telephone switchboard office, and houses on the other. The street between the two sides of the village measured about 50 feet wide, which should have been plenty of room to carry out the proposed attack, we figured.

The road through town had a slight dip in it. In other words, as you approached the town from either direction you went down a slight incline until you got to the center of town, then the road sort of leveled off for a few feet giving the road the shape of a shallow bowl—something that was absolutely essential for our plan to work.

The game plan was to place the hayrack at one end of town headed toward the other end. With the hayrack filled level with good dry hay, we would set it afire and start it down the incline.

The plan was for the blazing missile to progress to the center of town where the road leveled off, then from the momentum gained coming down the incline start up the incline out of town. If we had planned the invasion precisely, it wouldn't have quite enough speed and inertia to make it out of town so it would roll back to the center again and once again head up the incline to its starting point. It would finally run out of steam (Okay, sparks, fire and hay) and come to rest right in the center of town, making it look as if the entire town of Strong was a blazing inferno from a distance.

By this time, the plan included the knowledge that the volunteer fire company, if necessary, would arrive, put out the blaze, and no harm would be done other than a slightly charred hayrack. We would have the bragging rights as the greatest Halloween pranksters who ever lived in Strong, Maine.

Unfortunately, we overlooked one very important detail that should have been considered with hundreds of others during our month-long planning phase. Although we secured the hayrack's tongue well off the ground so that it wouldn't drag, we hadn't prevented it from swinging right to left, or left to right.

The first pass or two went according to plan, but on the third trip up the incline headed out of town, the tongue made an abrupt hitch to the left turning the front axle and wheels with it. We knew we were in bad trouble as the blazing rocket headed straight toward Mr. Leonard's hardware store.

By all rights, the town should have ended up as a big pile of ashes and the four of us sent to make license plates at Thomaston State Prison.

What happened next has to be considered as the eighth wonder of the world—or at least another one of the greatest miracles ever recorded.

It seems Pearly Whitmore (yup, the "Pearly-the-Pig" Pearly) was making his second cider run of the night into the county seat and shortly after impact arrived into town with his mode of transportation, another Model-A pickup loaded with gallon-jugs of cider. Seeing the inferno, Pearly swerved his pickup toward the blaze. He then parked it a short and safe distance away and then started heaving gallon after gallon of delicious apple cider onto the fire. Later, according to Pearly, he had no choice since what he saw when he rounded the hill into town looked like the great Chicago fire all over again. Only much smaller, of course.

The only chance to conquer the beast before it roared across town was to drown it in cider, Pearly figured.

The culprits, myself included, had taken refuge behind the Masonic Hall on top of the hill behind the post office where we could watch all the up-coming excitement.

However, the unexpected turn of events changed things considerably. Seeing Pearly all alone and possibly risking his life for a prank we pulled—never mind sacrificing his valuable cargo to save the town—proved too much for us. We just pitched right in and gave him a hand. We too, after all, were just out returning from a harmless night of trick-or-treating and came upon the scene just as had Pearly. At least that could be our story if we were questioned why we were one of the first ones on the scene. Even then, we proved that outlaws, however young and harmless, often return to the scene of their crime.

With our help and most of the cider, the blaze was finally quelled enough so it was brought under control by the time the volunteer fire company arrived. Pearly was the hero of the day for saving the town, an honor he surely deserved.

As for the hayrack . . . let's just say that except for the steel rims around the wheels, not much more was left of it.

Chapter 16

The Rest of the Story

Donald and Joan reside in nearby Livermore Falls, Maine, and are cousins of a close friend of mine. A few weeks back my friend invited me to go along with him for a visit to Donald and Joan's home.

It should be understood that although this couple is happily married with children and grandchildren, they began their lives in two different worlds. To begin with, Donald left Livermore Falls at a young age and was enrolled in the Perkins School in Boston. Here Donald would get his formal education from elementary through high school. After graduating, Donald attended a trade school where he studied and learned the machinist trade.

Later in life, after finishing trade school, Donald found employment at the Carr Company in Boston as a machine operator. It was my understanding that this company made metal stampings for automobile companies such as Ford and others. Donald would work for this company for 32 years, but due to the relocation of the company from Boston to Connecticut, Donald was offered and accepted an early retirement.

During those 32 years Donald was married, had four children—three boys and a girl. This marriage would eventually end by divorce, but Donald continued to take care of the children until they were old enough to go out on their own.

Some time later, Donald met Joan and eventually they were married and had two children, both girls. Then in 1975 while the girls were young, six and eight years old, respectively, they decided to move to Livermore Falls, where they built a beautiful home which Donald designed himself. Here they would educate their children and finally enter into semi-retirement.

Of course, this story would not be complete without a little background on Joan. She was born in Chile, then came to the United States on a scholarship and also attended Perkins School in Boston. It is of interest that while in Chile she, at one time, was an interpreter for Helen Keller. In fact, it was Ms. Keller who assisted with and helped make it possible for Joan to come to the United States and attend the Perkins School.

After completing three years of schooling in the U. S., Joan returned to her native land of Chile for a while then moved back to America permanently. Here she found employment with an insurance company and worked there until her marriage to Donald.

To make this story complete, a few things must be known about their move to Livermore Falls and their activities after they arrived there. In addition, we must not forget they both supposedly were entering into semi-retirement.

Donald furnished his entire basement with woodworking tools, machinery, and specialized equipment that he had designed and built. This fully-equipped workshop would provide everything needed to manufacture a variety of wooden crafts, household items and an assortment of the most beautiful clocks imaginable.

Most of the items he manufactured were made from kiln-dried hardwood and he would purchase a variety of species from places such as Bethel Furniture Stock or Andover Wood Products. His workmanship and accuracy with wood was equivalent to that of a fine Swiss watch.

Now 79, Donald works daily at his shop and enjoys a visit now and then from folks such as my friend and me.

Joan worked for many years in the school system and more recently as an interpreter for migrant workers in the area. She is active in public speaking at churches and other civic functions. Presently, she works at home knitting mittens and other apparel from the luxurious wool of the alpaca, a relative to the llama.

So why have I chose to tell this story? After all, many children leave home at an early age, attend specialized schools in other states or countries, and find jobs just like Donald and Joan did.

So, too, do couples get married, have children and grandchildren and provide for them just as the Donald and Joan have. And finally, often time you'll find other people like them who use their God-given talent to enrich not only their own lives but the lives of others.

Now this totally inadequate and short version of the stories of their lives does not and cannot begin to tell the extraordinary accomplishments of these two remarkable people. But one must understand that this is the way they wanted it. So once again, why have I told this story? . . . Because the Perkins School's full name is the Perkins School for the Blind; and yes, both Donald and Joan are totally blind.

As Paul Harvey would say, "and now you know the rest of the story."

Chapter 17

The Story of Norman

Norman is truly another one of the good guys. In fact, although many characters in this book have been given that distinction, Norman really stands out as a loyal friend.

Most everyone has one true and loyal friend. That is, if they are a friend like Norman, who has been my most trusted friend since I first built a modest camp on the north shore of Moosehead Lake in the early 1970s.

Rarely do I go "up-ta-camp" without inviting Norman to come along. There are many reasons. For one, Norman just loves to fish. Another is his love of the outdoors and his willingness to help out with the tough work of maintaining the camp.

Although Norman is one of those fortunate individuals that is blessed with excellent health, he unfortunately did lose sight in one eye, and by all accounts there should be no humor at all in that.

Strange as it might seem, however, this is not the case with Norman. In fact there is lots of humor associated with this loss of sight. For some unknown reason, Norman refuses to avail himself with eyeglasses even though many, including myself, believe that would help him considerably.

Now Norman, with all his virtues, can sometimes be a trifle stubborn. He would not seek any help for his eye and, admittedly, he does manage quite well without full sight. He does, though, make mistakes now and then. Some of these mistakes can be very humorous, but still nothing will convince our friend that eyeglasses would be a tremendous help to him.

That is, except for the time we were invited to supper at the camp to the north of mine. (The Chainin' guy is to the south). It seems the owners of these three camps often have one another over to supper now and then to exchange and, of course, exaggerate fish and deer stories and other happenings in their lives.

On this particular night, Norman was visiting my camp and we were both invited to supper. For purposes of this story we'll call the owner of this camp Ron. After a few refreshments it came time to have supper and we all sat down to an initial bowl of tossed salad. The main meal was going to be spaghetti with a wonderful meat sauce Ron makes.

Ron also puts up pickled beets and applesauce every year and brings both to camp to enhance his meals. This meal would be no different, with a large bowl of applesauce placed to Norman's left and the pickled beets to his right.

Ron serves his spaghetti on a separate platter, with the sauce in another bowl so everyone can put as much sauce as they want on their pasta. With the spaghetti platter delivered to the table, Ron announced, "Go ahead and dig right in!" He then went back to the stove to retrieve the spaghetti sauce.

With the platter of spaghetti placed closest to Norman, he does just that and heaps a generous helping of spaghetti onto his plate. Before Ron can return with the sauce, though, Norman has already blessed his spaghetti with more than a cup of applesauce.

When Ron approaches the table with the bowl of sauce and sees what Norman had done, he says to Norman: "By gorry, I knew you guys liked my applesauce, but putting it on spaghetti—now that's a real compliment."

Since no one else had seen what Norman had done, once we heard what Ron said, the camp walls nearly blew out from our gut-bustin' laughter.

Anyway the camp's resident-weasel had another great meal thanks to Norman. But perhaps most important of all, Norman now has his name placed with a long list of many who have made honest mistakes and given a lot of laughs over the years to the three owners of camps on the northern shore of Moosehead Lake.

Chapter 18

The Crazy Antics of a Guy called "Shrimp"

Where do I start with this guy? I suppose we could start by telling the story of him raising a bull calf in his cellar, and then having to butcher him right there because he got so big he couldn't get him out. Yup, that was a bundle of laughs, especially cleaning up the mess.

Or I could start by relating one of the many escapades this guy would go through to stay ahead of the law. But no, we'll pick a different story that made him another true "character."

"Shrimp" came rightfully by his name, being not much more than a few inches over five feet. Still, in spite of his small size, he made up for it with the crazy things he would undertake and surprisingly accomplish.

Imagine if you will this little guy coming into the local restaurant and making an entrance of a guy more than 6-foot-6. That is to say, here was a guy who would brag at the top of his lungs, for hours on end, of his antics to outwit the local sheriff or state trooper during his most recent caper.

And what might one of his stories entail? Well many of them were tales of his talent at thievery, although he never considered it as such. You see, Shrimp owned and operated a 10-wheeler dump truck and contracted to haul waste wood and other waste material to the dump for many of the western Maine woodworking plants when they were operating.

Somehow perfectly good items and/or materials found their way onto his truck before it was fully loaded with waste items. Now, according to Shrimp, he never knew how these items got there, but surely they were too damaged or scratched up to be returned to the plant where they came from. Still, on the other hand, they were too good to throw on the dump. This seemed to create quite a dilemma for Shrimp, but because of being the good guy he was, the items eventually found their way into half the houses in town.

My first-hand experience with Shrimp occurred from two separate occasions. One was an invite with a neighbor from Massachusetts who put on a once-a-year outdoor croquet party and hot dog roast. He always invited Shrimp, who kept him entertained during the entire party with his antics.

The story of the bull in Shrimp's cellar really put the neighbor into a state of uncontrollable laughter. However, the details of my encounter with Shrimp had nearly the same reaction.

Early one evening a while back, Shrimp showed up at my door. He had obviously been into the sauce, which was somewhat of no surprise. What was a surprise was his story that followed.

It seems he had gone off the road a ways up the hill from my home, crashed through the guardrail and head-on into a tree. "My wife is hurt," he said. "She's bleeding real bad from a gash in her head."

"Good Lord," I responded, "I'll call the ambulance and sheriff's department."

About that time his wife made her appearance at my door, covered with blood and, obviously, as inebriated as Shrimp. Now more concerned than ever, I went to use the phone.

"Whoa!" they both hollered together. "No cops, no ambulance, no nothing, just take us home."

Anyway, they convinced me not to call anyone; his wife maintained she wasn't badly hurt and to take them home. I agreed under one condition: That we get his wife to the hospital to be checked out.

Since Shrimp was in no condition to take her, the only transportation was my wheels—I was left with the job. With a towel wrapped around her head and instructions not to fall asleep, we headed for the hospital.

Two hours later, Shrimp's wife emerged from the ER, her head completely enveloped in bandages. With a handful of pain medication and written instructions, we left the hospital with no word from Shrimp.

As we entered the house we found Shrimp in my recliner watching television. Beside the recliner were the remains of Shrimp's supper. He had gotten in my refrigerator, made himself a couple of sandwiches, and found some soda and chips. Then he finally blurted out, "How's the old lady?"

The climax of this story was his convincing the law that he had gone off the road to miss a deer. Since the deer had lived because of his good turn, perhaps the state would pay for damages to his pickup. Well, I don't think that happened, but I do think his insurance took care of a lot of the damage.

This is just one of the many stories that could be told of Shrimp. Sometimes the story of all the contraband buried behind his house will be told. On second thought . . . perhaps that story should wait until he passes on!

Chapter 19

Kids Do the Darnedest Things

Remember when Art Linkletter had a TV show called "Kids Say the Darnedest Things?" Well, this story is a little different as it is titled, "Kids *Do* the Darnedest Things."

I thought it would be a great tribute to my son, Rick, who died from a heart attack at the young age of 39, to tell some of the humorous stories about when Rick was a youngster.

Sometimes it is very difficult to remember the humorous and joyous things that happen in my life after the unspeakable loss of a dear son. Such is the case with this story, as Rick was not only my dear son but my best friend as well. Still, it is important to set that sorrow aside for a while and concentrate on the joy Rick brought into not only my life, but the lives of his mother, sisters and others as well.

Rick and I began our father-son friendship at a very young age. He was always underfoot at a boat business we once owned, and if he could find anything to entertain himself, regardless of the consequences, that is where I would find him.

This first episode would set the stage for what was

coming down the road for me for many years to come. At the boat shop we had constructed an I-beam boom that swiveled approximately 180 degrees on top of the boat-shop roof. Along this I-beam traveled a dolly with an electric hoist suspended from it. The electric hoist was actuated from two ropes that hung about a couple of feet off the ground. Pulling one rope in one direction would bring the lifting mechanism up to unload boats and pulling the other rope would lower them to a desired location just by swinging the boom to that location.

Although I got to the boat shop early every morning, Rick wasn't far behind. He'd just entertain himself with various mechanical things until the rest of the crew arrived. One thing that was never necessary was to give a whole lot of thought to where he was or what he was doing. That is except when he was literally "underfoot" so to speak.

On one particular day, with the usual hustle and bustle of the boat shop going on, Rick was not only "not underfoot" but he was nowhere to be found. That is until a faint cry for help was heard outside of the building. That cry was undoubtedly from Rick, but once outside he was still nowhere to be seen.

"Up here," came a shaky voice.

There the little bugger was, suspended more than a dozen feet in the air. He had taken the hook from the hoist and hooked it into the collar of his jacket, pulled the appropriate rope and was experiencing a ride usually only found at a county fair.

Needless to say this prompted a good tongue thrashing, but it also brought laughs from that day to present.

Twice a month, Rick and I would travel to Bucyrus, Ohio, to pick up boats from a manufacturer out there. We would leave early in the morning, as it was about a 14 hour to 18 hour ride, depending on the weather and traffic. Before we had traveled 50 miles, Rick would be sound asleep with his head in my lap. Some 12 or 14 hours later, I, too, would need a little "shut eye," so I would pull into a rest area and make preparations for the both of us to sleep an hour or so.

On one particular trip, just as I was about to fall into dreamland, I felt something pulling at one of my earlobes. I realized it must be Rick, as he was probably hungry by now. But I figured that if I pretended to be asleep, he, too, will drop off again. A minute or two later, however, I felt an object go up my nose and realized it was Rick's finger in my nose. Still I pretended to be asleep. Then one of my eyelids is pulled wide open and I now have no more defenses.

"I can't sleep," comes a tiny voice.

"Are you hungry?" I asked, which of course was the wrong question to ask a three-year-old who had been riding and sleeping for a dozen or more hours. After a cheeseburger, milk and fries, we are once again on the road and within an hour or two will be entering Bucyrus.

After another 15 minutes or so, I looked over and

Rick was sound asleep again. Now I have a decision to make: do I grab a couple of hours myself or do I get to Bucyrus, get loaded, and catch an hour or two then.

I chose the latter so I was not running late when I arrived.

With the boats loaded, with one on a rack over my pickup bed and two more on a specially-built trailer behind the truck, we were off once more. But within an hour or so, I could hardly keep my eyes open so figured it was a good time to catch a few winks since Rick was already—once again—sound asleep. I pulled off into a rest area and quietly put a pillow that I carried, between the window and my body and immediately fell asleep.

After a mere 10 or 20 minutes of rest, I felt the same earlobe being pulled, only this time it felt like something was trying to dislodge it from the side of my head. Again, it is my little guy, only this time he says, "Daddy, I gotta go pee."

Now, you don't fool around when a toddler says he has to pee. I did what was necessary, and just in the nick of time, I might add.

With that chore competed, we were on the road again and I figured I'd wait until he was asleep and try the same plan as before so I could get at least an hour or so of sleep. An hour goes by, then two, then six or eight or more, and this little bundle of energy was still awake. So I kept driving until he was once again ready for a fuel stop.

I fed him well, figuring this would surely put him

to sleep again so I could get a couple of hours myself. Eureka! It worked. And now was my chance, I thought to myself as I again pulled off the road. And again, in no time I was sound asleep.

An hour later, now with two fingers buried deep up my nose, I hear, "Daddy, Daddy! I gotta go poop!"

You don't waste any time with this distress call either. So once again we are settled back in the pickup, but by then I was wide awake so I figure I might as well keep driving and make record time getting back to the boat shop. In another four hours, I drive into my yard with the little guy once again sound asleep. Once parked and ready to unload, Rick woke up and discovered we were back home.

"Oh boy, Daddy," he says, "now we can go to the park pool after work to feed the ducks."

This same trip was repeated time and time again even after Rick started school. The only difference was that as he grew older, it required a few more stops for food. Those trips are memories I will cherish and live with until Rick and I meet once again in the hereafter.

Chapter 20

Priceless Memories Never Before Told

By now it should be obvious that some memories are priceless. We all have them. Some we may want to share, while others we may choose to keep locked in our hearts and souls. What one does with his or her memories is a matter of choice. What a person does with them often depends upon the circumstances associated with those memories.

With this next story, I was torn between whether it should be told or locked in the personal vault that we all have within our being.

Although the exact time, date and place are unimportant, this story took place during my youth. In fact, I was in adolescence and just really beginning to learn and understand right from wrong.

It was during this particular time that I took up a friendship with a fellow a few years my elder. For the next two to three years, the two of us lived a life of dishonesty, deceit and by all other definitions of our actions, crime!

Thanks to my "buddy," I would learn how to steal without getting caught and live a lie by never telling the truth about where I had been, what I had been doing, or whether I went to school.

As a young boy, barely 12 years old, I was well on my way to a life of crime. So what saved me and got me back on the straight and narrow road to again live an honest life? Well, many things happened, but probably most of all—as strange as it may sound—it was my conscience. And what was it that put my conscience in gear to finally get me straightened out?

Well, this life of crime was really getting too far advanced for me to fully comprehend or understand. I had advanced to watching my friend break into a hardware store under the cover of darkness and steal two 22-caliber pistols. For my dedicated surveillance, I was given one of the pistols with several boxes of bullets. It was after two or three days of serious meditation and thinking that I realized this was totally wrong and that I must do something to get myself back on the track of honesty.

What I did was absolutely bizarre, and my solution to making things right again only continued me on a path of dishonesty. With the gun concealed, I walked to a nearby location, still within town limits, and disposed of the gun over a pipe railing and down an embankment. Then I crawled over the railing and down the embankment and retrieved the gun again.

I went to the police station and presented the gun to the chief and told him that during a routine walk by the railing, I looked down the embankment and spied the gun. I would then tell the police chief that I went over the railing and down the embankment to get it.

This explanation may have seemed a great idea,

but it was still dishonest and I knew it. On top of that, I must have done a terrible job explaining my story (lying) because in a very short time the chief learned the truth to the whole gun incident, as well as several other thefts.

I was now in deep trouble—and my "buddy", teacher, and leader was in even more trouble. So much so, that eventually he was sent to the Maine state prison in Thomaston, where he died years later.

As for me, the police chief had made tentative arrangements for me to be admitted to Father Flanagan's Boys Town in Nebraska, where I was to spend the rest of my teen years.

Lucky for me that never happened because the more investigating the chief did, the more he realized that I may have been as much of a victim as those who had been stolen from. Nevertheless, there were conditions that went with this so-called pardon and I followed those conditions to the letter.

Even when I moved to Strong, although I engaged in a few boyhood pranks, I also worked faithfully in the mill-owned hotel as a chore boy until I graduated from high school, and then in the toothpick mill until I was drafted into the U.S. Army.

So why has the vault been opened to tell and expose this story after so many years? I'm not even certain I have the answer to that question other than to say it just seemed time to "fess up." Perhaps I hope that by telling the story, it may turn some other young person around who may be headed in the same wrong direction.

And what makes the memory of this story priceless? ...This "turnaround" was accomplished not only through my God-given conscience but from the compassion of a dedicated police chief in a small Maine town.

Chapter 21
The Story of Clyde

During my years in Strong, I did many things to get my life back on track. Besides working in the hotel, I worked for a friend's father, named Clyde, who owned a farm on the outskirts of town.

Clyde was an easy-going mentor and wonderful man who taught me and my friend (Clyde's son) much about the ways of farming, which included working in the woods. On weekends, my friend and I would go with Clyde to help cut wood—white birch cut to 4-foot lengths used in the local mills for toothpicks and other items.

It should be mentioned that my friend also had a sister who was not only beautiful, but was also very popular in school. She was in my class but I found out that a neighbor had his eye on her, too. However, this story is about Clyde and not pretty girls. Although by then, I was really starting to take an interest in them.

I began to look upon Clyde as somewhat of a father figure. Although my prime reason for working was to earn money, the time spent with my friend and his father, Clyde, was just an added bonus. And of course, once again, we must not overlook that seeing my friend's sister now and then was something I looked forward to as well.

As time went on, my friend and Clyde became an important part of my life. In fact, much of my off-time and spare time was spent with them. We would do everything from trying to catch muskrats in the nearby farm pond to cranking up an old Model-T Ford that made its residence on the farm

Incidentally, for those of you who do not know, Model-Ts had to be started by hand-cranking. During this cranking process they also sometimes kicked like a mule. That is to say, the engine would misfire in such a way that it would turn the crank in the opposite direction or rotation. The force of the crank turning in the opposite direction could lift a 300-pound man clear off his feet and send him completely into *Painsville.*

In fact, cranking that monster was the reason I first injured (actually dislocated) my right knee. Really, this incident was worthy of perhaps not a Purple Heart, but certainly a "purple crank" that I could wear on my lapel for the rest of my life.

All through my days in Strong, I would keep an association with my friend and his father. Even after I graduated from high school and took a job in the toothpick mill, my association with Clyde remained.

By this time Clyde had downsized his farm and taken a job in the toothpick mill as a maintenance man. Although this next part of the story may be unpleasant for many to read, it is such an important piece, it needs to be told.

In time, I had graduated to actually operating a toothpick lathe in the mill. This was hard work and required a bit of skill to learn how to get the most yield from the wood being used to make the toothpicks. Later, automatic devices were engineered to help lessen the hard work associated with this job. These automatic devices would actually install a new stick of wood and remove the spent piece from the lathe, something the operator had to do manually for many years.

These devices were controlled by air-over hydraulic cylinders which in turn were put into motion by push-button controls operated by the worker. The framework of this new equipment would probably weigh in excess of three tons. The frame consisted of one frame sliding inside another much like the drawers of a file cabinet. The hydraulic cylinders would produce the power to move the top frame inside the bottom section or frame.

It was actually the top part of the frame that automatically picked up a stick of wood and advanced it into position in the lathe to make the wooden ribbons for toothpicks. It should be understood, the clearance between these two frames (the bottom stationery one and the top sliding one) was minimal.

On one particular day, a malfunction occurred as I was operating this lathe with this new device. The top sliding frame had picked up a stick of wood and positioned it into the lathe as it was supposed to, however it stayed or stuck in that position and would not return to pick up another stick as it was also programmed to do. A maintenance man was summoned and my friend and mentor Clyde arrived to correct the problem.

Clyde took a few minutes to access the malfunction, and thinking he had it analyzed, reached down inside the bottom stationery frame and actuated a limit switch that was normally actuated by the top fame on its return trip. At that very second the top frame bolted back like a bullet out of a gun giving Clyde no chance or time to remove his arm. Clyde's arm was now nearly severed except for a few sinews that remained hanging between the wrist and elbow.

What had just happened and what would take place for the next few minutes, was a most horrifying ordeal to witness. In fact, I will take the memories to my grave. With Clyde's arm laterally severed between his wrist and elbow, the device was now stuck in that position and Clyde can not get free from it. Blood was streaming everywhere, and unless Clyde was freed very soon, he would surely bleed to death.

Every available piece of equipment was used to try and pry the top section of frame from Clyde's severed arm, but with no success. Eventually, another maintenance person arrived; it may have been my uncle who somehow de-energized the hydraulic cylinders, which allowed the top frame to move ahead once again.

Clyde was rushed to Franklin Memorial Hospital in Farmington, about a half-hour's drive from the mill, where a Dr. Brinkman, previously an Army surgeon, saved Clyde's arm by attaching it back on—a miracle surgery if there ever was one.

Admittedly, the arm wasn't a pretty thing to look

at, but in a little more than six months, Clyde was once again able to lug a 10-quart pail of water from his house to his barn.

I have many memories of the people who influenced my life. Some of those memories are humorous and some are educational, while others are sad. This one happens to fall into a category all of its own. In fact, I can find no words which can adequately describe those memories from this story or this time in my life. I can say, however, that I am grateful to have had my friend and his father in my life.

Chapter 22

The Delightful Stories of Ah-Ah and Dampy

Can anyone possibly imagine having an aunt who was also his/her grandmother, and a grandfather who was also his/her uncle? I'll give you readers some time to think about that one.

First, an explanation: my aunt, who was my father's sister, eventually married my mother's father, who was my grandfather. So if you think about it, this also made my aunt–my grandmother, and my grandfather–my uncle, at least by marriage.

Although this isn't the significance of this story it made for a good bit of conversation over the years. The significance of this story is as the title indicates—the delightful experiences my sisters and I shared with these two wonderful relatives, who substituted for the parents who were unable to raise us. Indeed, they were special. It may be difficult to explain just how wonderful they both were or how profoundly they affected all our lives.

It's not exactly clear how Ah-Ah and Dampy got their names, but probably because the youngsters in the family could not yet say "aunt" or "grampy" clearly and so the abbreviated versions just stuck with them.

Regardless, these are the names these two relatives went by for their entire lives. Every evening, usually right after supper, Ah-Ah and Dampy made the half-mile walk to visit me and my sisters. The only exceptions were inclement weather or when we'd had fried onions for supper. It seems the smell of fried onions and Ah-Ah didn't get along well—they actually made her sick. So whenever she detected the smell of onions, they turned around and walked back home.

This ritual would last for many years until we children became too big to hold and cuddle any longer. Each night they would rotate their affection, showing their deep love for each child, so literally there was no child left behind.

Of course, the affection and love was the greatest gift given to me and my sisters. However, material items also rated high on the list. Now we're not talking about toys, expensive bicycles or the like, but clothes such as hand-knit mittens, socks and scarves. Why, my sisters were even blessed with complete outfits of dresses, coats and sweaters, all made by hand from scratch and thin paper patterns.

I even recall one outfit that included matching capes and hats. A more talented seamstress, knitter, or crocheter as Ah-Ah never existed. Her homemade quilts, bedspreads, tablecloths and doilies were works of art. Even some of these crocheted items, such as tablecloths and bedspreads, were made as one single piece. Her talent at making strawberry, blackberry, raspberry, and blueberry preserves from freshly-picked fruit was extraordinary. On one occasion, I counted more than 500 jars of these delicious preserves sitting on a shelf in their root cellar. And it may be of interest that each of these jars were sealed with paraffin wax, which incidentally made for excellent chewing when the jar was emptied and the wax was finally ready to discard.

Obviously, one of Ah-Ah's and Dampy's favorite pastimes was picking wild berries. Often times they would take me and my sisters along for the enjoyment, which included a picnic lunch around noontime.

Although their art and speed at picking overshadowed us by 10-to-1, it was never an issue. Regardless of what might be in our containers when it was time to leave, we were always complimented on how well we had done. Both Ah-Ah and Dampy were excellent gardeners. The grounds around their home were immaculate, with well-groomed rock gardens and flat-rock paths winding though hundreds of plants and shrubs.

In the mist of all this greenery was a totally flat and cleared section, which served as a croquet area. Dampy was extremely organized, with everything in his garage and cellar perfectly situated and within an arm's reach. His cars, always second-hand, looked as though they were brand new.

When we got older and the nightly visits became less frequent, a new ritual began which we initiated. Walking three miles to and from school was commonplace, and even walking the three miles home for lunch was not unusual. After school, in the afternoon, the children usually made a routine stop at Ah-Ah and Dampy's. The same love and affection was always given and usually a delicious raisin– or date-filled cookie rounded out each visit.

Yes, these two dear relatives helped shape our lives and most certainly they made a much happier childhood for each of us.

Without a doubt, their love helped stimulate my conscience when that conscience was so desperately needed at the age of twelve.

Chapter 23

A Story for Children Who Don't Believe in Santa Claus

When my sisters and I were young, we were told, mostly from older kids, that there really was no Santa Claus. Yet even today, I believe that Santa is with us all throughout our lives—if you choose him to be.

That is to say, that no matter what others say or do to convince you otherwise, it is your beliefs that really count. If you, like so many young children, have been taught that this jolly fat man, with an enormous white beard and dressed in a brilliant red suit, is the one responsible for your good fortune at Christmas time, then keep those teachings with you throughout your life. This, along with other teachings about the meaning of Christmas and the accompanying holiday season, can be an inspiration to you if you want them to be.

In our home, the talk of Santa coming usually began sometime after Thanksgiving. Often, especially with the two relatives featured in the last story, it was another means to show more of their affection for my sisters and me. Unfortunately for some, it was also used as a tool to help keep kids in line until the day of Santa's expected arrival. You all know how that works: you misbehave, and the threat of Santa not coming unless you straighten up, usually did the trick. Actually, it worked quite well, too, at least through the month of December.

However, the arrival of Santa was much more than that. Much more. He was someone we could think about and make a whole lot of plans around, not only at Christmas time but throughout the entire year. To help with this idea, perhaps you'd wanted a special item for a long time—say, a pair of skis, a sled or maybe that special doll—however, that special item could have been very costly. To help keep the disappointment of not being able to have it right away, there was always the hope that if we were really lucky, Santa would bring it at Christmas time.

Along with this aspect of Santa, there were many other things to think about. Plans must be made about what to leave him for his lunch—after all, perhaps the other folks that he visited might not be as generous as we tried to be. We were certain Santa would be hungry by the time he arrived, so we planned the old standby of cookies and milk. Although at times, a piece of pie was substituted in place of the cookies; it was never a surprise when the next morning only the crumbs remained.

Finally, after participating in all the school and church pageants, the big day would arrive. More often than not, Santa had left the special gift that had been wanted for some time. How delighted we would be to receive the special gift and then tell our close relatives and friends of our good fortune. It had been, after all, perhaps nearly a year since we had first asked for the special item.

But then again, there were also disappointments. That special present might not be there. Perhaps Santa had not received our letter or perhaps we hadn't behaved well enough. Whatever the reason, there was a deep feeling of sorrow when that special present wasn't discovered under the tree on Christmas morning.

So how did we handle this disappointment? Surprisingly well. Looking back, everyone did a marvelous job of explaining why that present could not be there that particular Christmas. But perhaps even more importantly, we were taught other lessons: to cherish the substitute present with the same enthusiasm as though we'd gotten the gift we had hoped for, and finally, not to give up hope that if it was meant for us to have that special gift, it would someday present itself.

And so, you young folks who might be reading this story, this is why I have always believed in Santa Claus as well as God and, for that matter, perhaps a guardian angel.

If it is meant to be, whatever is hoped for may some day present itself—perhaps in a different way, in a different form, or a different light. All you must be able to do is recognize its appearance.

At least for me, that belief and the ability to recognize those appearances have undoubtedly given me a more fulfilling life.

Chapter 24

Taken for Granted

After talking with one of my friends not long ago, I learned another valuable lesson in life: that I take entirely too much for granted.

"Do you take too much for granted?" my friend asked me.

"I know *I* did," he added. "That is, until I realized what I was doing. Now I have changed my ways.

"Follow me here for a moment and I'll explain," he continued. "Most every day we interact with a variety of folks, some we know and some who are strangers. It's all about how we communicate or somehow associate ourselves with these folks, especially on a daily basis.

"For example," he said, "if we make trips to local stores, the post office or perhaps a town office, we expect those working there to be open at their regular hours. We also expect, to some degree, we will be waited on promptly and courteously and our desires and needs satisfied.

"Isn't that correct?" he asked me. "Don't we take all of this for granted?"

"Sure," I answered, "but isn't that what they are supposed to do?"

My friend continued. "Although you may be technically right with your thinking, have you ever really thought about it? The folks working in those businesses, stores, or agencies are people just like you and me. They have needs, sicknesses, or family crises just as we do. Yet do we give their needs an ounce of consideration? I think not. Usually we expect the places to be open on time to take care of our needs, and if they have a problem they should take care of those problems so they can be available to take care of ours."

"But that just comes with the territory," I said.

Again the man said, "Sure, that kind of response may be okay, but aren't we really taking a little too much for granted? Think, if you will, of all the things being done for you by family members—say, your wife, husband, daughter, or son. If we are the man of the house, aren't there certain things our wives just inherently do for us on a daily or weekly basis? Perhaps getting our meals, doing our laundry, or keeping the house in order. Or perhaps it might be waiting on us when we could just as well wait on ourselves.

"Don't we just take these things for granted most of the time?" he asked. "Now, please don't misunderstand me. I don't mean to insinuate that we may not be grateful and appreciative. I'm just asking, however, shouldn't we acknowledge those many tasks and personal services from time to time instead of taking them for granted?"

He continued when he realized that neither I nor

his other friends were convinced of his logic. "I will try one more time and then throw in the towel.

"Consider the airline industry if you will. Many of you may have had to fly recently. Now anything taken for granted with this mode of travel or these "birds" and you're in a world of hurt. In fact, in this case, it is wise to be more considerate of yourselves and to take absolutely nothing for granted unless you have no qualms about replacing your wardrobe, sleeping on the floor in a major airport, or perhaps taking an unscheduled flight to Timbuktu.

"Ah ha!" he exclaimed with a bit of joy in his voice. "I can see by your faces I've finally gotten my point across: it just makes a difference who is being taken for granted, doesn't it?"

Chapter 25

Woodshed Strikes Again

First, let's make it clear that our friend Woodshed featured in our first story is really not a bad guy. Some of the things he may do or get involved with may be bad, but usually they can be forgiven—although not always.

Again, although it's no excuse, Pickwick or Ballentine ale have a lot to do with Woodshed's escapades. Most of the trouble he gets himself into can be traced back to his partaking of too much of this beverage.

For the most part, Woodshed works every day and gets to work on time. He does, however, have a bit of a secret that contributes to many of his mishaps at work. Fortunately for him, no one has discovered this secret so far, although I believe it's only a matter of time before someone catches on.

That episode may come from the result of this last mishap, as it's obvious this one won't be taken lightly. Visualize Woodshed if you will, climbing aboard a forklift he has operated at a local lumber company for some time now, and literally demolishing a waste conveyor.

Could it be he tapped into his trusted Cabala's quart-size thermos one too many times? This is, after all, the only logical explanation, especially since he just got into his truck and left work without saying anything to anyone. He really didn't have to say anything, as the crushed conveyor disrupted production from the mill to the extent that the entire mill had to be shut down.

When the mill owner discovered what had taken place, he got into his pick-up truck and drove straight to Woodshed's house. Here he found Woodshed sitting at his kitchen table with another quart of Pickwick nearly expired.

"You worthless skunk," the mill owner hollered. "Tear down my conveyor then come back here to celebrate your stupidity. You ain't getting off that easy this time."

With that said, he grabbed Woodshed by the collar and literally dragged him outdoors and into his pick-up. Once in the truck, Woodshed began to regurgitate about a half-gallon of smelly Pickwick, along with most of an Italian sandwich he must have eaten for his lunch. Now Woodshed really goes on the defensive by throwing up again, this time probably his breakfast and what looked like last night's pea soup. Then he announced he had just fired himself so the mill owner was wasting his time taking him back to the mill.

With the pick-up smelling like an open cesspool and Woodshed covered with two previous meals, they head back to the mill. By that time, the mill owner had had just about enough when he said to Woodshed, "If you can tear down my conveyor and put my mill out of commission, you are going to help put it back together."

Although Woodshed continued to maintain he had fired himself, the mill owner presses on to his mill and when they arrive, he washes Woodshed off with his fire hose.

By now Woodshed had sobered up somewhat—the hosing off probably helped considerably—and he was now a little more cooperative. In fact, he pitched in and helped reconstruct the conveyor as if nothing had happened. It took half the night with six or eight men working until after midnight, but finally the conveyor was operational once again so the mill could start-up on time in the morning.

The next morning, Woodshed was back on his forklift as usual. His first task of the day was to place his trusted Cabela quart thermos under a back wheel, run over it a dozen times until flattened, and then nail it to the mill bulletin board.

cAp

Finally, his secret booze container, at least this one, would never again get him in trouble.

Chapter 26

More Thoughts About Friends

Thus far, many of the stories in this book have been about friends. However, to give a slightly different take on this subject of friends, I want to focus on my own personal view of friends and friendship.

If we are lucky, we all have friends. They come in all sizes, colors, shapes and ages. Some are close; some are distant. Some are best friends, while others are dear. If we are really lucky some are both dear and best.

Then there are lost friends. Those may be the ones who we dread having the most. Some we may have lost to disagreements, while others may have passed on to another life.

Then there may be relatives such as a sister, brother, cousin or spouse who may not only be a relative but a best friend as well.

And finally, to some perhaps, it is God who is considered their best friend.

Regardless of the number of friends one has, or their status, friends for the most part are important to all of us. A wise man once said, "If we can count the number of true friends on one hand, a major part of our lives has been fulfilled."

Another wise man said, "If a man or woman is without friends, then you have someone who has an empty spot in their life."

So there are a few questions we should ask from time to time: How much time and consideration do we give to those friends? And are we being thankful that we have them? Isn't it a distinct possibility that at times we put more value on other things that have no life, real meaning, or human value than we do our friends?

I'm afraid that I may be guilty of that at times, but in my own defense I hope that it's kept to a minimum.

On the lighter side, why is it we seem to connect with some folks more than others? Of course, one reason is that we just enjoy their company and being around them. We might like their wit, their personality or wisdom. It may be their ardent concern for us and our families. Or, for that matter, it could be a dozen other things—some of which you may not be able to put your finger on.

Whatever the reasons, doesn't it really make little difference? Just the mere fact that they are friends and you have them as such, is really the important thing isn't it?

A final thought and a tiny bit of personal philosophy: perhaps it is time for us all to let a friend know how much they mean to us.

Chapter 27

The Story of a Pig Named Dolly

There is no doubt our friend Pearly was the last word when it came to raising pigs. He not only knew what made them tick, but he also understood their mannerisms and what prompted some of their stubborn streaks.

Perhaps most important of all, though, was his ability to understand how they could think almost like a human. Some say Pearly even understood pig language. That is to say, he understood what a pig was saying just by the tone of their squeals. Well, I took that one with a grain of salt, although I did witness some remarkable things take place between Pearly and his pigs.

Still, there was someone else in my life that had a knack for raising pigs. That person was my father, who came in a close second to Pearly with his knowledge of pigs. Although he certainly didn't have the knowledge that Pearly had knowing all the niceties of pig behavior or most certainly what each different squeal meant, my father still knew how to raise monstrous pigs. Often they would tip the scales at well over 600 pounds at butchering time.

Of course, both my father and Pearly thought they had their own secrets to raising pigs. Pearly's secret really wasn't a secret at all since he told everyone that pigs have to know you love 'em, and furthermore, to never let them know the real reason they are being pampered like a prize French poodle in a New York dog show.

As for my father, his secret was much different and "totally off the wall." His children were his secret. How so, many must be wondering? Simple: have the kids make a pet out of them—which we did.

Why, a thoroughbred Shetland pony wouldn't have gotten as much attention as my father's pig did. Each one of us children would take turns riding on this pig all over our parents' one-acre farm for hours on end.

Unfortunately, this had a downside for my father. All this activity with the pig, who we named Dolly, hindered our father's best efforts to fatten her up.

When Dolly should have been sleeping and storing fat, she was gallivanting all over the dooryard and up and down a hill that led to our home.

Fortunately, a solution was found for this little problem: skim milk was a by-product that was either given away or dumped into the sewers at that time. In those days, there were places called creameries where the farm milk was processed much like it is today, only the milk taken from cream had no value.

It was here where skim milk was given to my father, who in turn force-fed it to the pig. In other words, pigs will eat continuously if there is something in their troughs. My father would leave a 55-gallon drum of a mixture of the best grain he could get his hands on along with a generous amount of skim milk and table scraps—better known as swill.

When Dolly wasn't being used for our personal entertainment or finding ways to escape from the confines of her pen, the trough was always kept full by us. In fact, at times the pig would be so stuffed it could hardly move, to say nothing about trying to get up. All it could do was raise its head barely off the ground and either give a pig burp or squeal from a likely bellyache.

Dealing with our pig wasn't all fun and games, though. Dolly, like all pigs, also had an ornery streak. Pearly would have known what caused our pig's tantrums, but my father never had a clue. All we knew was that every so often the pig would go on the war path, and like Pearly's pig, tear down clothes lines, then root-up flowerbeds and our father's prized rhubarb patch.

After being satisfied with her re-arrangement of all the landscaping around the grounds of our humble home, Dolly would then disappear down the hill to visit neighbors up to a mile away.

What that pig put us and our neighbors through trying to get it back up the hill and into the pen is nearly beyond description. To put it in some sort of prospective is to say that if this had been a human causing all this absolute chaos throughout the neighborhood, every law enforcement person available would have been summoned. In addition, a "Wanted Dead or Alive" poster would have been nailed to every telephone pole and a crew from the "funny farm" would also have showed up with straight jackets.

Eventually, the pig would either become worn out, hungry for the pig gourmet meal waiting outside the pigpen, or just plain satisfied with driving the entire neighborhood and its owners nearly bonkers.

For some unknown reason only Pearly would understand, the pig would finally return home and start acting again like the normal pig that gave rides to us children and eating like a pig—pun intended.

When it came butchering time, everyone except my farther had some unannounced regrets and reservations. Behind the scenes a few tears were shed, as a member of our family—Dolly—had finally been sentenced to pig heaven.

Chapter 28

The Story of Uncle Nelson

Every year during mid-summer when my sisters and I were youngsters, our father would host a family reunion. All the relatives, including his four brothers and two sisters and all of their families, would attend. One brother named Nelson would come all the way from Mooseup, Connecticut, where he owned and operated a laundry.

Uncle Nelson was the youngest of the five brothers and he was also a strange sort of bird. Perhaps it seems disrespectful to refer to Nelson as a "bird." Yet, there is no other way to describe him. To give you some idea about this guy, many years ago the Red Sox had a pitcher named Bill Lee. They called him Spaceman because of his "off the wall" and crazy antics. Well, Nelson's crazy stunts and sometimes-stupid practical jokes would put Bill Lee's reputation to shame.

Nelson would always be the last to arrive and the first to leave the reunion. If his visit lasted 30 minutes after his arrival, then something must have gone wrong with his planning.

My Uncle Nelson just loved to fight—not with his fists but with his words. He was a master when it came to arguments and was usually engaged in one within ten minutes of arriving at our family gathering. No matter what the subject matter might be, Nelson's opinion was always the opposite of his brothers. This was especially true when arguing with my father. In all the years Nelson made an appearance, not once did he and my father ever agree on anything.

Yet, for bystanders that didn't have to match wits with him, he was well liked. It was probably something like a situation with a physical bully one may have encountered in grade school. As long as this bully didn't beat the tar out of you, you seemed to like him. But if the tides turned then you hated the guy.

Still, Nelson was clever. He had a knack of making his opponent "see red" each and every time they butted heads. A favorite maneuver of his was to use the young children to enhance his point or to put the point across so no response was possible.

For example, my cousin Arthur and I would mingle freely among the grownups at the reunion. Nelson just loved using Arthur as an accomplice to help him win his confrontations. He would look squarely at Arthur, then wink in a childish fashion and say to my father, "Good gosh bro, even a seven-year-old kid knows that much." Or he would make his point other ways by saying, "Even Arthur agrees with me on that, right Arthur?" Then he'd smile, which would really make his brother's blood boil. When my father sent Arthur away to rejoin other kids, family members knew things were going to come to a head very quickly between the brothers.

More often than not, it would end by my father ordering his brother off the property and telling him never to come back. Strange as it may seem, Uncle Nelson would always returned the following year and continued to do so year after year.

Evidently, the 350-mile trip from Connecticut had been well worth the drive just to once again "lock horns" with my father, even though it was for only a mere 30 minutes.

In other stories passed down about Uncle Nelson, some were hard to believe yet they would seem to fit him to a tee. He was, after all, a practical joker who acted out his antics with no consideration about what the consequences might be.

As already noted, Nelson owned and operated a laundry business that took in laundry from ordinary folks as well as commercial laundry from hotels and motels. Of course, this required much larger machines to take care of the bigger loads.

Although it was never an issue at any of the reunions, Nelson had a reputation in his hometown, of once in a while taking a few more nips than he should. Like any business owner, Nelson had quite a few friends who joined him with his after hours "nips or sips."

One night, a friendly threesome had a few too many sips or nips, causing one of the friends to fall asleep from not only the spirits but also a hard day on his backhoe. Nelson's number two friend suddenly posed the question to Nelson, "What would happen if we gave old Tom there the ride of his life in that big ole dryer over there?"

Without giving it a second thought, Nelson grabbed the top part of Tom and instructed his other friend to handle the feet. Before starting the machine, the second friend asked, "This won't do him any harm will it?"

Nelson responded, "Oh, he may have a little extra headache, but other than that he should recover in a day or two. Besides I'll leave a few sheets and pillow cases in there to soften the ride."

It's hard to know if this story is really true, but it was reported that this poor guy couldn't get on his backhoe for more than a week. How long he was left tumbling is unclear. However, he was bruised from head to toe and we're told he never again took another drink with Nelson!

When my cousin Arthur (Nelson's unknowing family reunion accomplice) got older and learned to drive, he took Nelson fishing on a man-made reservoir outside of a town where they lived. As they were fishing, Nelson left Arthur for a while and started fishing in a brook that ran into the reservoir— where fishing was illegal. There were "no fishing" signs everywhere.

In a short while, a game warden showed up and asked Nelson what he was doing. Since Nelson was always one to think rather quickly on his feet, so to speak, he replied, "I'm just fishin."

The warden then asked, "See that sign over there?"

"Yup," Nelson responded, "they're all over the place.

"What do they say?" the warden asked.

"Danged if I know," Nelson said as he kept right on fishing. "I can't read."

Arthur maintains that Nelson actually convinced the warden that not only couldn't he read, but that he was a little retarded as well. The warden reportedly escorted Nelson back to the reservoir and made a final comment to Arthur: "Young man, you should really take better care of your uncle so he doesn't get himself into trouble. I just caught him fishing on a closed brook. Now I'm letting him off this time but make sure you keep a closer eye on him so it doesn't happen again."

Although Arthur had no idea what had just taken place with the warden, he knew his uncle Nelson pretty well. He also knew the less said the better, so he meekly responded, "Yes sir, I will." All of this time Nelson was enjoying himself beyond words. In fact, all the while Arthur was being lectured, Nelson was having a hard time keeping a straight face. Nevertheless, once again Nelson had succeeded in being Nelson. Here he had nearly gotten himself in some serious trouble and, by lying through his teeth, was able to put the blame on someone else.

Not only did these stories in all probability actually happen, like putting his friend in a dryer or the story about him having a fully operational "still" in his laundry basement to make his white-lightening. The rumor about his transporting one of his four dead wives across state lines, in his own van to avoid the cost of a hearse, to have her buried in her native state of New Hampshire, could also have been true.

Chapter 29

One Road In and Out

As previously mentioned, I have been blessed with many different types of friends during my lifetime. One such friend was Jim.

Jim was another of my friends who held many occupations and jobs during his life. One was being a school teacher, and another was selling a variety of hardware items throughout Maine. In fact, he traveled from Kittery to Fort Kent peddling his wares.

One day Jim was traveling along the coast on Route 1 and, as he often did, veered off the main road to visit a small town or village. Usually getting to and from these towns was easy since there was usually only one road into and out of these towns.

After discovering that there was no hardware store in a particular town, Jim stopped and asked an elderly lady, "Which way to Ellsworth ma'am?"

Since the lady pointed down the road Jim had just driven to get into town, he responded, "But I just came from that way."

"Look yung fella (Jim was well into his 60s then) ah've lived in this heah paats all ma life," she said in Maine coastal speech. "They's one way inta this heah town and they's one way out. Thataway goes ta Ellswoth and thataway goes ta tha oshen, and unless ya got a boat waitin' for ya down theah, ya best turnaround an go tha way ah jus' tole ya."

As Jim was about to turn around and thank the lady, she added, "O-yeah, ah forgot ta mention, ya could swim . . . 'cept tha watas afuld cold this tima yea.'"

Chapter 30

"Roughing It"

Many of my stories deal with my own experiences with some of my friends during my life. This story happens to be another one of those experiences.

Camping has always been a big part of my life. Even traveling cross-country by covered wagon in the pioneer days was a form of camping—only it would be a little difficult to convince anyone of that back then.

As a teenager in Strong, a typical camping trip was to take a couple of loaves of bread and three pounds of salt pork and paddle a two-man kayak to the island at the end of Porter Lake for a three-day stay.

Things have changed just a trifle since those days. In fact, perhaps "trifle" is a totally inadequate word to use to explain the extent of the changes that have taken place. To put the changes in a little more perspective, perhaps a story about a camping trip with a friend a while back will help.

Soon after I got the invite from this friend, I immediately went to the storage area for my camping gear and retrieved a two-man pup tent, a Coleman lantern, cast iron cooking utensils, a sleeping bag, and other items usually taken on a camping trip.

While waiting for my friend to arrive the next day, my mind would repeatedly wander back to those wonderful days and nights spent back on that island in Porter Lake. Sleeping on the bare ground using pine boughs as an insulator along with a couple of handmade blankets in the middle of October was my idea of camping. Repeatedly eating salt pork sandwiches for three days was all part of the enjoyment of the experience.

My friend arrived right on time and I couldn't believe my own eyes. As he came to a stop in front of my house, all I could do was look in total amazement at all the fancy camping stuff my friend had gathered up for our trip. It somehow seemed to quell my enthusiasm just a bit. Oh, I still wanted to camp, but ole' L.L. Bean had gone off the deep end just a bit with some of the modern camping gear of today. I was speechless for a full minute.

"What in the world is this?" I finally quizzed my friend.

"Like it?" my friend asked.

"How can I like something I ain't had a chance to look over?" I asked back.

"Go ahead and look her over, and by the way, put all those antiques back in your barn," my friend advised with a chuckle. "This week we're goin' camping in style."

He wasn't kidding.

After returning most of my "antique" gear back to its original storage place, I began to look over a monstrosity on wheels. Before I had a chance to even go inside, I blurted out, "I thought we were goin' campin' not joinin' the ranks of those who couldn't build a camp fire if their life depended on it."

"Simmer down," my friend fired back. "Don't knock it till you've tried it!"

"Okay," I reluctantly agreed. "I'm just darn glad it's you who has the payments and not me."

With that said, my friend said, "We only go this way once; better make the best of it while we're here."

As I continued to look the beast over, I asked another question. "This sucker must be thirty-feet long. How in the world are we ever going to maneuver it around all those trees where we usually camp?"

"Wrong again," my friend said. "Thirty-five feet and has all the 'bells and whistles.' As for trees, this baby will turn on a dime."

Once I had thoroughly looked over this mobile home on wheels, I continued my questioning. "Where'd they build this, down at Keiser Homes in South Paris?

My friend's camper/mobile home had everything from a gas stove with an oven to a toilet and shower with tub, not to mention a stereo system that sounded like the New York Philharmonic.

As we finally got underway, I thought to myself: *If this is "camping" then our next fishing trip will be going to Shop 'n Save and filling our cart with choice haddock.*

Still keeping my thoughts to myself, I wondered if perhaps I was just envious—until my friend announced,

"Yup, in 60 months I'll own this thing and once we get used to it, we'll never want to crawl into a tent ever again."

"God forbid," I said. "If this spoils us for real camping, you're not getting that party that you wanted at your wake. Yes sirree, your funeral will be duller than that ole' double-bitted ax you've been using to cut those hornbeam trees in your back yard."

Now, I admit I might be a bit old-fashioned and perhaps even quietly a bit envious, but really, who ever heard of going camping and sitting on a real toilet that flushed, then be able to wash with hot or cold water, not to mention enjoying an oven that baked like the best Hotpoint ever made—then after all of that, nearly freeze half to death from an air conditioner powered by an on-board generator?

My goodness, this Hilton on wheels even had a television that had better reception than my three-year-old Zenith. As for getting around trees, evidentially someone sold him a bill of goods on that one, so to speak. Why, an area the size of a football field was needed just to park the thing.

Still, all in all, most everything turned out okay except for a part of his TV antenna that still hangs on a low pine-tree limb.

Oh yes, one other thing: apparently there is a special procedure required when using the toilet. Although there will be no details given, this much will be said, "knowing how to clean out an outhouse sure came in handy!"

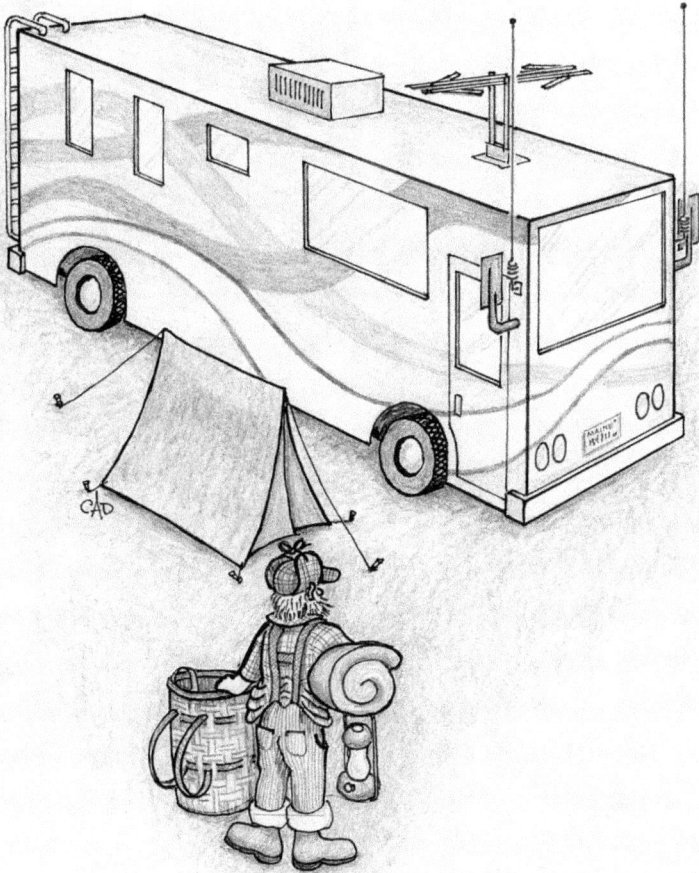

Chapter 31

Embarrassing Moments with a Friend

Although I cherished the good times from the outings I had with my friends, not all of them went off without a hitch. This story is about one of those outings; hopefully there will be a lesson here for everyone who owns a boat.

I have a friend who lives down around the town of Gray who had just bought himself a new boat a few years back. Actually, the boat was used and so it was only new to him. Since he was eager and anxious to put it into the water, he called wondering if I would be interested in christening it with him. In addition, the Royal River Blue Fish tournament was starting that weekend so he thought perhaps we could "kill two birds with one stone."

The largest striper yielded a top prize of $4,000, and the largest bluefish caught would bring a prize of $1,000. We would share the winnings if we were lucky enough to catch one of these beauties.

It should be known that the chances of winning the "big one" is slim at best, as you are up against some of the best salt water anglers in the entire state of Maine and probably Massachusetts, too.

However, as with any contest, it is still a matter of

chance. That is with the exception of those who live right near or on the ocean. It is believed those guys hold better cards than those of us who lived inland.

The day finally arrived for the big christening. For those who own a boat it will be no surprise to understand there are certain rules and procedures used at launch time. In fact, there are certain rules and procedures that should be followed even before launch. Violate any one of these unwritten requirements and you might find yourself in a "world of hurt." These unwritten rules actually apply more than ever when it comes time to launch, especially if there are several other eager fishermen also waiting in line.

Of course, the same rules apply when taking the boat out of the water. Only now there will probably be one or two lawbreakers who've been into the "sauce" and their patience, unlike their bellies, may be a bit thin.

What I'm implying here is that everything must be in order so the boat does not linger at the dock any longer than absolutely necessary. The ultimate goal is to avoid any unnecessary interference with other boaters. With that understood, the boat is then backed into the water and set afloat, then moved to the far end of the dock where the owner's fishing buddy ties it off.

Once the boat is launched, the vehicle operator hurries to park the trailer and attempts to get back to the dock in record time. If everything has been properly taken care of ahead of time, this procedure will usually go off like clock work and there will be no other unhappy fisherman.

Now, while all of this is taking place, the fishing buddy (in this case, me) makes preparations to start the engine by priming the bulb in the gas hose to make certain there is gas going to the engine.

As I was doing so, I noticed the transom well was about half full of water. Since this was his first time in the boat, I gave it little thought until I noticed about two inches of water over the soles of my sneakers.

Another clue: there was water seeping up from under the rear seats.

I said to myself, *This can't be right. Could my friend have forgotten to put the plug in?* Instinctively, I went to the dash and actuated the bilge pump switch. Unfortunately, there was no telltale sound of a bilge pump from under the rear deck.

Now, there was little doubt the plug was left out as the entire floor was covered with more than three inches of water. About this time my friend is making an appearance and walking down to the end of the dock where the boat has been tied off.

"Hey friend," I said, "you wouldn't have forgotten to put the plug in the boat would you?"

The answer was what I feared, and now it was not only panic time, but also the Battle of Alamo, Custer's Last Stand, and the Battle of the Bulge all rolled into one.

If I attempted to detail what took place during the next half-hour there is a serious question of whether anyone would believe me. With the crisis finally over, the boat back on the trailer, and my friend a nervous wreck, I finally asked him, "Is this why you got me up at two a.m. this morning, so we could get on the river by five and be fishing shortly after?"

Looking at my watch, I continued, "Apparently you miscalculated since it's now 9:30 and water is still bellowing out the drain hole. I'd say we'd been better off if we'd put in about four yesterday afternoon."

With my friend's face still buried deep in his hand and no response to my questions or comments, it was obvious he was one unhappy camper—or in this case— boater. "Look," I finally said to break the tension and disappointment, "things could have been a whole lot worse. At least the boat didn't sink and instead of twelve guys up for murder, you've got twelve thank-you cards to mail out."

I added, "That alone is something to be thankful for. I mean, really, think about it. You are still alive to fish another day, and what a story you've got to pass on to your grandchildren.

In truth, it was I who had the story to tell, since it's doubtful my friend will ever breathe a word to anyone.

Chapter 32

The Other Side of the Story

It goes without saying that humor in one's life is not only a blessing, but it can be something that remains part of a person's life no matter how many years pass. Humor also can be used in a multitude of ways as time goes by, including when visiting with friends and family we may not have seen for some time. Or it may serve to lighten up a meeting with new acquaintances, or perhaps be helpful at a party or outing at a hunting camp or on a fishing trip.

Yes, humor can be an important part of our lives. Often times it helps shape our personalities or even help to make us a more likeable person to some degree. Still, we understand life is not all fun and games and probably that is the way it should be.

So I will now take a short break from my humorous memories and concentrate on some of the more serious parts of my life.

The setting is still in Strong; the time is still years ago when I first came to the small, rural town. I did not arrive in Strong simply by happenstance, for it was another uncle who helped make that possible. This uncle was instrumental in getting me an interview for a potential job at the mill-owned hotel. The job would include a place to live if I were lucky enough to be hired.

So what was it like for a young, unsophisticated boy to enter this huge elegant building known as the Strong Hotel to interview for this job? Scary. In fact, just climbing the number of steps that led to the entrance of the hotel filled me with apprehension.

Once inside the carpeted hallway, to the right was a lovely well-furnished sitting room. The resident doctor's office was located to the left, and a dining area could be seen straight ahead down the hallway.

A few steps down the hallway on the left wall and opposite the sitting area, was a huge oval-shaped mirror which gleamed with evidence it had been washed and dusted daily. As I walked down the hallway past the mirror, a woman who I would later learn was the head chambermaid met me and introduced herself. She asked me to walk down the hall into the dining area and then on into an impressively-equipped kitchen to meet with the head cook. This lady would be the one interviewing me for the job.

By this time, I was so overwhelmed with the beauty and elegance of that most magnificent place that I nearly lost all hope of ever being able to work there. I wondered what my uncle had done to put me such a position; surely they would be looking for someone of better stature, experience and, perhaps above all, an older age.

Nevertheless, I had the interview, which incidentally, I thought went quite well considering how nervous— and out of place—I felt. In fact, I did well enough for the head cook to explain what the job entailed and give me a full account of what my responsibilities would be.

I was expected in the kitchen at 5 a.m. sharp, the cook told me, and would proceed to fill all wood boxes—two in the kitchen for the combination gas and wood stoves, and the one in the sitting room, or parlor, for the fireplace. Next, I would be expected to remove all garbage and take it to the holding area outside to the rear of the hotel. I also had the option of having my breakfast before starting my daily chores. When I had finished with those jobs, I would then remove all dirty hotel laundry, such as sheets, pillow cases and towels, to the basement laundry area and then replenish the linen closet with fresh laundry.

By that time each weekday, I would be going off to school. However, after my lessons were done, I would be expected to return directly to the hotel to fill the wood boxes again and take out the day's garbage. I would then check with the chambermaid for any other miscellaneous jobs she might need help doing.

This job would have a title of "chore boy" and it paid $10 a week, plus room and board. The head cook then explained if I would wait a few moments she would get the chambermaid to escort me through and around the hotel to further understand what more this job involved.

As I waited for the chambermaid, I couldn't help

wondering to myself that they surely would not spend so much time with me if there wasn't some chance that I would at least be considered for the job.

The chambermaid's tour lasted nearly an hour.

As it turned out, I indeed got the job and it was there at the Strong Hotel where, in a few short months, I felt that nearly half the occupants of the hotel had adopted me. Everyone was wonderful and kind, and I was even encouraged to join the usual after-supper adult discussions of the day in the beautiful sitting room. It was also there in the sitting room where I learned to play cribbage, which I did nearly every night.

HOTEL STRONG
STRONG, MAINE

Yes, from the compassion of a good-hearted police chief in another small town in Maine, I got what turned out to be the break of my young life. Had it not been for that police chief, who could have had me sent to a boys' reformatory school far from Maine, there probably would have been no Clyde, Charlie or Pearly stories.

This is not to say, however, that there might not have been other excellent opportunities elsewhere. But it is still difficult even today to imagine that they could have been any more enjoyable than the time and years spent in the Strong Hotel, in the woods of western Maine.

Chapter 33

More Stories About Life in Strong

It is often said that variety is the spice of life. When this phrase is used in the proper context, it is undoubtedly true. Now I'm certain we all had a variety of activities that we were engaged in as teenagers, and some of those activities stir priceless memories that we all cherish. Of course this book has already told many of them. Yet, there were many other activities or things going on years ago that are either unheard of today or for some unknown reason they no longer exist.

Once I had established a routine for my work at the hotel, I found I had time for just being a teenager. Of course, girls were being thought about with some degree of interest, but not to the point where they were at the top of my priority list. It would only be a matter of time before this would all change.

For now, though, guy things such as working in my spare time for Clyde and spending time with Clyde's son, along with target shooting rats at the local dump, hunting small game, fishing, camping and tinkering on old cars remained some of my favorite activities.

Strange as it may seem, I still found time for some other fun things that haven't been mentioned and they might very well fall into the category of "no longer existing" or "they have fallen by the wayside."

So, if I were to ask anyone today if they wanted to go "suckering" in the spring of the year, would they know or understand what I was talking about? Perhaps there are still some who would know, but chances are that most people would not. In the spring, suckering was one my favorite nighttime pastimes, as soon as the water level dropped in the brooks. I would join Woodshed—who was not yet married nor had yet acquired the name Woodshed—would board his poor excuse for a vehicle and, along with another friend, head for New Vineyard just east of Strong. There, a favorite suckering stream, or brook, bordered the small town and finally went under a bridge directly into the center of town.

Many folks know a sucker is a bottom-feeding fish that has little or no value for any purpose. This is especially true when it comes to eating the critters. Why, a pine board soaked in cod liver oil would probably taste better than a sucker.

Regardless, during the spring they migrate out of a nearby pond at New Vineyard and go up a particular brook to spawn. For some reason, like the smelt, they travel up brooks at night. Often times the brook at New Vineyard would be filled from bank to bank with them and this is what makes for absolutely great suckering.

The idea is to wade up the brook among the slippery devils with a flashlight or lantern and spear them as they swim, without ending belly up yourself. The spear is a three-pronged device with barbs so the fish cannot come off once it has been speared. Perhaps a better way to describe the spear might be to say if a hay pitchfork had the tines straightened then barbs put on the end of the tines and was reduced to about one third its size, you'd have an ideal sucker-spear.

Since suckers have no value, a person might ask: what is the purpose of spearing them? Believe it or not, it was just a lot of fun, not to mention a challenge trying to stay upright. But saying they had no value wasn't absolutely true.

Remember our friend Pearly? Well, this was his secret for growing great gardens. Like the Native American Indians, Pearly would use all the suckers we could spear (and that was many, many) for fertilizer for his garden.

However, our friend, who was later called Woodshed, had an even better use for them. —It's worth noting that not everyone could be considered Woodshed's friend. In fact, some of the residents didn't like him very much and he knew it. So these folk would have been better served if they had had a little more tolerance for our friend's shortcomings.

After we speared suckers, we would put them in a grain sack until it become so heavy we could no longer stay upright on our feet. We'd then leave the sack full of suckers on the brook bank to pick up later. Then, with a new sack, we'd begin all over again. Many nights we would leave for home with as many as a dozen or more sacks of these suckers—pun intended.

Can anyone imagine the stink a sack or two of these suckers would make after a week or two, or even a month or so? Well, there were a few residents of Strong who didn't have to imagine because they knew first hand, especially after Woodshed and his friends had concealed a sack or two under their front porches or tied a sack securely to the frame of their cars.

After this last story about Woodshed, I wouldn't be surprised if people wondered why I continued my friendship with such a character. For a fellow such as me, who was trying to put my life back together in a new location, it would seem Woodshed might have been the last person I should have been associating with. Perhaps I haven't been entirely fair to Woodshed with these stories. Although there is absolutely no question this fellow was most certainly a character, practical joker, and a bit of a drinker with a few other questionable traits and habits, he was still one of the so-called "good guys."

First and perhaps foremost, it should be understood that Woodshed was a few years older than me, and even with all his faults, he never once offered me a drink or invited me to join him having one. Although we did establish a relationship and engage in activities like suckering and deer hunting, or traveling together with other friends to the nearby town of Kingfield to see Woodshed's girl friend, never did he entice me to engage in any of his antics.

Indeed, I may have been present or witness to some

of Woodshed's crazy pranks, such as planting a bag of suckers under some residents' porches, but the "dirty deeds" were always done solely by him. Still, I admit I genuinely enjoyed watching Woodshed's defiance of his mother and grandmother's rules and regulations and I just loved to ride in his 1931 Chevy jalopy.

There is one more final comment that must be made about Woodshed: He was a true and loyal friend who never did me any harm, nor did he ever influence me in any way to do harm to any*one* or any*thing* . . . in addition, as with some of the other stories in this book, although they're based on actual happenings, they may be exaggerated—just a wee bit— to enhance the happening.

In summary, the memories I have of time spent with Woodshed will always be cherished.

Chapter 34

The Murder of a Chainsaw

I have often been invited to various friends' camps on Moosehead Lake, especially on the north shore, but I am not one to take advantage of an invitation without helping out with some of the many chores that come with owning a camp.

On one particular fall day, shortly after arriving with my host, we realized there must have been a severe windstorm that blew across the region. After getting settled into camp and having a usual lunch of cheese sandwiches and Campbell's tomato soup, we began to assess the damage.

The wind had indeed taken a toll on the camp site. Armed with chainsaws, axes, peaveys, and everything else except a skidder, we went to work cleaning up the mess. We started on the north side clearing the mountains of downed brush, then began working on the bigger wood debris. While my friend limbed the branches of a rather large hemlock, I climbed up on top of the trunk of the tree and proceeded to cut the butt off about 10 or 12 feet from its roots.

Now, even a greenhorn cutting the first section of a tree knows to stand on the ground, not on the tree—

especially not on the butt end that's being cut off. My brain
must have been idling, since I was now sawing off the tree
while standing on top of it—on the butt end, no less.

As the chainsaw made its way completely through
the wood, the butt end suddenly jolted upright like a
shot-out-of-a-cannon. At that point, I was propelled
through the air—like a shot—with the chainsaw still
running. I can see that our destination, mine and the
chainsaw's, was going to be the lake.

With my host watching in fear and wonder, I land like an astronaut's space capsule, chainsaw and all, in the lake. My friend heard the "gurgle, gurgle" sound of the chainsaw sinking into the water and was thankful the machine was now disabled.

My friend is now in a panic about my own condition. Just as he got ready to dive into the frigid lake to rescue me, he sees a hand and part of my arm emerge and wave frantically. Now sure that I had escaped rather unharmed, he gave up the idea of freezing off *his* buns to save *me*. He figured the worst that could happen to me was a little hypothermia and a possible drowned chainsaw.

I finally made it back to shore, but had to wait a day or two before rescuing the chainsaw, which never again cut another bush, tree, or log. I had sent it to its death and was grateful I hadn't done the same thing to myself.

No, not my best experience in the woods, but I survived. So did the ten-foot stump, which still stands upright as a memorial to a guy who took an unscheduled ride through space on a chilly October day, ended up in the northern end of Moosehead Lake . . . and lived to tell the story.

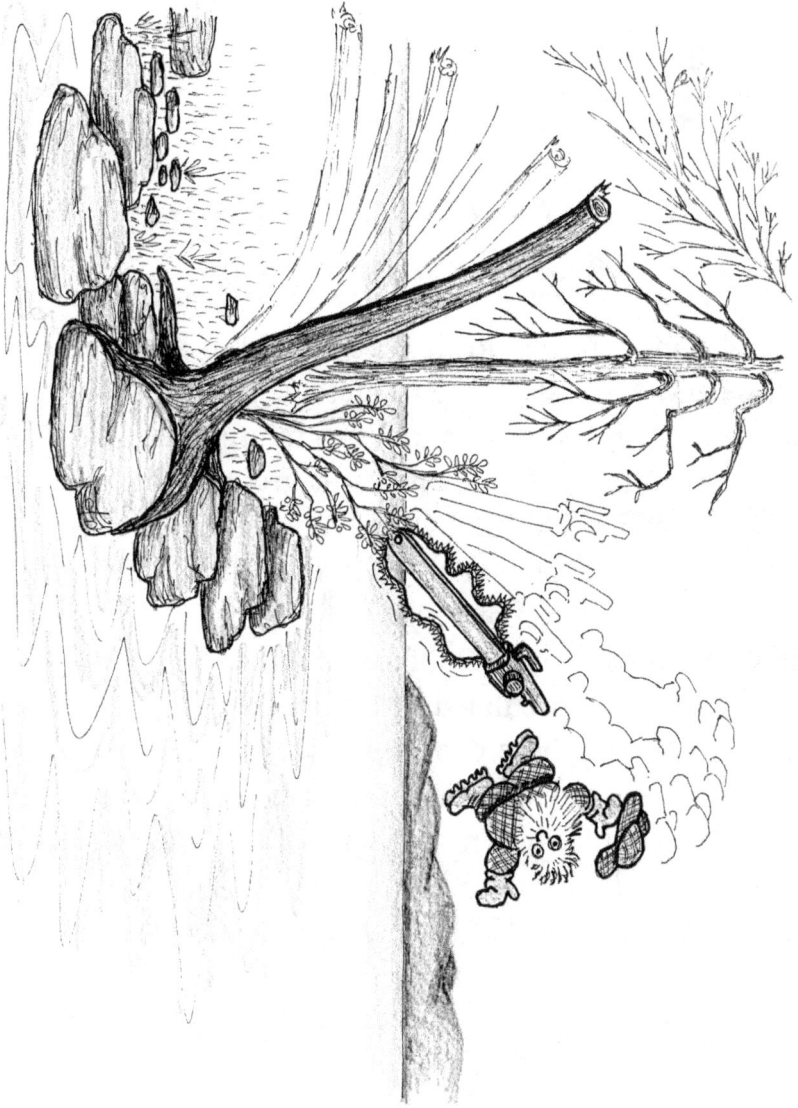

Chapter 35

Another Murder: This Time— A Choice Igloo Cooler

Friends in the North Woods tend to be somewhat close and often do things together. In fact, a favorite pastime for my friends and me is hunting together.

To abide by Maine laws, our group of hunters had adopted a ritual whereby the hunting group—usually five or more participants—spread out in different areas and communicated by legal walkie-talkies. From time to time, we alerted each other to our location.

On this particular day, I decided I would take up a popular site where deer had a habit of crossing. As I drove my pickup to the area and was attempting to park it, a voice came over my walkie-talkie. "Deer going to cross behind your truck!" I heard.

I answered back, "Soon's I get my rain gear on, I'll check it out."

"Look, stupid," came the same voice, "you ain't got time to do anything but get out of that truck. Those deer will be there at any moment."

As I slipped out of the truck, I noticed a head with horns peering out of the hardwood whips a few feet from my truck. I quickly loaded my gun and then trained the scope crosshairs on the deer's head. Just as I was about to pull the trigger, the buck bolts out from behind the whips and leaps toward the road a few feet behind where my truck was parked.

The deer was so close to me that it now filled the entire scope's viewing area so that I could not find a vital spot on the animal. Before the deer could make another leap and disappear into the evergreens on the other side of the road, I squeeze off the single round I had loaded into my rifle. I was sure I had hit the deer, since the scope was still completely filled with deer hair when I fired. "Got him," I announced over the walkie-talkie as I walked toward where I expected to either find the deer or a profound trail of blood.

What I found was absolutely nothing—except huge hoof marks buried deep in the mossy soil and continuing off into the dense woods across the road. "Impossible," I muttered to myself.

As I waited for my hunting partners to arrive to see my buck, I wondered what to tell them. Surely this crowd wouldn't believe the story of what actually happened, but what else could I possibly tell them but the truth?

The response from my heartless so-called friends was predictable: they believed my story about as much as if I had claimed the deer weighed 400 pounds.

Dejected, the least I could do was break out the lunch I had prepared and perhaps the food would nurse my wounds enough that the guys would invite me hunting again.

As I grabbed the Igloo cooler that I had packed, I couldn't believe my eyes: the cooler was sticking about a half-foot above the tailgate, directly in the line of fire . . . and the corner of the cooler was blown off to expose a gaping hole.

At least I felt my hunting partners would now understand my story, but instead, I was tagged (pun intended) with the nickname "cooler killer."

Someone I thought was a friend teased me to the point that he told me he would mount a set of deer horns on the cooler and attach it to a huge pine tree located directly behind my camp.

That hasn't happened yet, but you can be sure: it will!

Chapter 36

The Ride of a Lifetime

After my episodes with the Chainin' guy (Yes, the same one from Chapter 10), we became good friends and shared other adventures. Sometimes, our wives would even join us.

On one particular winter day, my friend and I, and our wives, decided to take a 107-mile trip around Moosehead Lake on snowmobiles. It was not an easy ride. First, from my friend's camp we drove north across the lake past Seboomook Campgrounds, then west to the Pittston Farm. From there, we took one of the many well-groomed snowmobile trails to Rockwood, another 25 to 30 miles. Here, we entered a marked trail onto Moosehead Lake and traveled east across the ice to the base of Mount Kineo. We then picked up the main ITS trail to Kokadjo and traveled on it for another 20 to 30 miles to another north-west intersection.

It was there, after turning left at the intersection, that we soon encountered some of the most beautiful snowmobiling terrain in all of Maine—a route that rivaled the trails around Rangeley Lake, or Aroostook County in the far north of the state.

The trails at the intersection would take us another 30 to 40 miles directly to Ed and Shirley Raymond's store in northeast Carry Plantation, as well as dozens of places in-between. Once we arrived at the Raymond's store, we were back home, so to speak, since we were a mere three miles to the Chainin' guy's camp.

Back at camp, everyone was exhausted. Unbeknownst to the two men, the wives had discussed us having supper together once they finished the long and snowy ride. But the Chainin' guy's wife realized she had made a tossed salad, but didn't have any dressing for it. Since another of my friends owned a camp not too far away, and I knew he always kept a variety of dressings on hand, I figured the problem was solved.

With the Igloo cooler in the rear carrier of my snowmobile, (yes, the same one I later murdered on that fateful hunting trip), I drove over to my other friend's camp and retrieved some salad dressing.

For some unknown reason, probably only known to the devil, I removed the Igloo cooler from the rear carrier, stashed some salad dressing inside, and then decided to drive back to my friends with the cooler sitting in front of me on the seat. I drove on the trail through the woods and, although it was well-groomed, it was narrow and included a few up and down knolls and corners to negotiate.

In fact, one corner is especially tricky to get around, as it is right at the bottom of quite an incline—a few hundred yards before the trail goes back onto the lake. Just as I was making the corner, I turned the handlebars with my thumb still on the throttle lever, which jammed up against the Igloo cooler sitting between my legs.

Unintentionally, I am about to set a new record for speed on a snowmobile. I feared the cooler was headed for the junkyard and I was headed for the morgue.

This absolute blazing missile must have looked like Jimmy Johnson or Jeff Gordon crossing the finish line at Daytona, as it plowed through alders, bushes and everything else in its path—finishing in a cedar swamp. From there, the machine climbed up a ramp that Mother Nature left behind during her last snowstorm. The snow had weighted down a huge limb on a hemlock tree until it lay on the ground and provided a natural incline-ramp for me and my poor snowmobile.

And climb it did, about six feet or more up the tree limb where one of my snowmobile skis finally wedged between another limb and the tree trunk. The engine was still running when it came to its final destination.

The debris field was nearly 100 yards long, which consisted of pieces of broken windshield, rear view mirrors, fiberglass cowling and other pieces of my personal gear—including a helmet, face shield, a glove, part of my face mask and even a faint blood trail. We found the trusty Igloo cooler the next day, complete with the salad dressing, about 20 feet away from the trail and the tree.

I was unhurt, but quite shaken by the ride. In fact, I was so shook up that I was unable to get the machine out of the tree, so I left it suspended six to eight feet off the ground and hobbled down the trail out onto the ice where I could now see the lights of my friend's camp.

As I hobbled into the camp looking like someone who'd just survived a train wreck, the questions began to fly from every direction.

Embarrassed, I wanted to fib about what had happened, but other than maybe telling them that, "While coming down over a knoll I was run over by a raging bull moose still experiencing the remnants of the rut," nothing else made sense. And seeing as there would be no moose tracks to be found—I told the truth.

Anyway, how was I ever going to lie enough to explain why my friend had to nearly cut the tree down to dislodge my snowmobile out of that tree trunk?

The big mystery—never solved: the machine's engine was turned off; by whom, I'll never know.

Chapter 37

A Story About One of My (In)famous Ideas

My wife was always a good sport. Oh, she had her times, but for the most part she pretty much went along with the "flow" regardless of the consequences.

As previously explained, spring around Moosehead Lake and its environs can be a trifle unfriendly. Experience can be a wonderful teacher. In fact, my wife and I took excellent advantage of some of those experiences.

To explain and give an example, we once stopped trying to go beyond the Seboomook Camp Grounds by vehicle when going to our friend's camp in the springtime. We learned it's better to walk in mud than snowmobile through slush and water over ice.

One spring Saturday morning (about two a.m.) we head out to Seboomook by vehicle then snowmobiled across the ice before the sun had come up enough to make any pools of water on top of the ice.

Now, it's important to know during this particular time that we had only a single snowmobile, so we rode double everywhere they went. The other significant thing to know is that my wife absolutely hated—

perhaps detested would be an even better word—getting wet during this time of year. That was precisely why we would head north so very early in the morning. If we got there too late and pools of water had begun to emerge, we would get soaked from the water flying off the snowmobile track and up over the rear of the machine.

Another fact: this is originally where the term, "Not a Happy Camper" came from, as my wife truly was not a happy camper whenever this happened. I suppose if one really thinks about it, having your backsides swimming in a sea of ice water might not be as pleasant as sitting in a tub of scented bath water at 90 or 100 degrees.

So I tried to be a considerate husband and would do just about anything to avoid getting her wet this time of year. Unfortunately, one weekend because of a late start, we didn't arrive at the campgrounds until nearly noon. Unfortunately, too, the weather was mild and the sun had already started making standing pools of water over the entire northwest cove.

There was no way my wife was going to agree to going across this nearly three square miles of what looked big enough to be an ocean.

As it was, I really had a dilemma, since I wanted to get to my friend's camp in the worst way, yet I had to give a whole lot of consideration to my wife's objections as well. What I needed was a way to keep her dry and therefore solve both of my problems.

Behind our truck seat was a 55-gallon drum of heavy gauge garbage bags that my son had given me for leaf storage. I had an idea, but I kept it to myself for a while before posing the idea to my wife. Under my plan, I would cut two holes in the bottom of one of these bags so she could put her legs through it, then have her climb into it so I could tie it off around her neck. Surely, this would keep her dry for the soggy 3-mile trip across the ice.

I was nearly an hour convincing her it would work. Why I had even convinced myself. By the time the dogsled was loaded and she was "suited up" looking like a giant human watermelon, the sun had melted even more ice; the lake was now covered with slush.

Now, as most snowmobilers know, slush and snowmobiles do not get along well, nor do they make for a good marriage. So I knew I would have to hit the ice with the throttle wide open and keep it that way all the way across the ice. Since the ice was still quite thick (more than a foot) there was going to be no worries about falling into the lake. The problem was avoiding getting mired in slush, as I knew that could be even more of a problem than getting a truck mired in mud.

Fortunately for me, I had kept an ace-in-the-hole. My snowmobile was a long track, high-powered Kawasaki, and once the hammer was put down on that baby, she would take on slush like a trooper.

Well, it finally came time for "take off" and as we headed off land onto the ice, the tachometer was red-lined at 6,000 RPM. As I looked back in my rear view mirrors, I saw water and slush flying everywhere. But we were maintaining a constant speed of about 30 miles an hour, only about half the speed the machine could travel on a hard-packed surface.

The farther we went and the closer we got toward our friend's camp, the more things began to go wrong. Luckily, the RPMs held at 6,000, but the speed began to dwindle. Also, my wife began screaming at the top of her lungs. But there was no safe way I could stop, as the dogsled behind us was already a huge mound of slush, and I had to believe her screams were just her enjoying the ride and from the elation of staying dry, (yeah, right.) Besides, if I ever stopped or lost any of the RPMs, we were going to be in one huge world of hurt. Obituary page here we come.

As we got closer and closer to our destination, it became more evident that we were going to make it, although the speed had dwindled to less than 10 to 15 MPH. The RPMs still held at 6,000.

"What a snowmobile!" I thought to myself, as everything was now caked with slush—not only the dogsled, but the running boards, skis, and especially, my wife, as I looked in my rear view mirrors. Could this be why she had been beating on my back for the last five or so minutes? Well, I would soon know as we were slowly approaching the front of the camp.

Normally, we would take the entire rig off the ice and up the incline to a few feet from the back door.

But not this time. There was just too much weight as everything, including me as well as my wife, was packed with slush.

As I was coming to a halt in front of camp, I again thought to myself, "What a great idea I had had with the garbage bag. Without it," I told myself, "she would not only be soaking wet but she would be furious."

Well, not only was my wife covered from head to toe with slush on the outside, the garbage bag had swelled to nearly twice its size from the slush going down her neck and filling the bag. The slush was now melted and turned into ice water. She was so weighed down with slush and water that she was unable to get off the machine. I couldn't believe my eyes, but I now knew why I was being nearly beaten to death during that wild and wet ride across the melting ice.

It was also obvious I had now gotten myself into "hot water" with my wife. (Actually, this time it was cold water.) She was not only wet, but she looked like a human sponge. There would be no way I could ever get her out of that garbage bag so I cut it open with a jack knife and it was like opening the gates of Hoover Dam.

Remember at the beginning of this story, I said my wife was, in most instances, a good sport. Well, compared to what could have gone on, she more than lived up to her good-natured reputation, as well as being a good sport. Was she mad, angry, and terribly agitated by the whole affair? Yes. But all and all, she was so glad to finally make it to camp, it quelled the anger a bit.

In spite of all that had taken place and once everything had been unloaded and dried off (including my wife), this was just another adventure. It was also a fun and hilarious time—at least for me.

Although it took awhile, my wife, eventually, was also able to see a wee bit of humor in this great idea that was supposed to keep her dry on a spring day at Moosehead Lake.

Chapter 38

The Loyalty and Love of a Devoted Wife

One day in mid-April some years ago, my wife and I decided to try to drive to our camp on Moosehead for a short stay. Spring is one of the worst times of the year to travel in that part of rural Maine, as getting stuck in a sinkhole is more the rule than the exception. It is actually almost a certainty, especially when trying to get into a secluded camp in springtime.

In Maine, we often say there are five seasons of the year—the fifth being "Mud Season."

On this spring day during the fifth season of the year, the inevitable happened about two miles from my camp when my vehicle suddenly came to an abrupt stop. When I got out to take a look, I found the truck mired up to the frame in a free-floating sea of mud.

With no means of communication, our alternative was to "hoof-it" to my friend's camp to get warm and meditate on our situation—which we did. He always left a key for me in case I got into trouble and needed to use his winterized camp. Once there, we came to the conclusion that the only way to get out of this predicament was to hike another three miles across the ice to another friend's camp at the end of the lake for help. These particular friends had spent the entire winter at their camp and they would be able to help us, before our names appeared in a local newspaper on its obituary page.

However, there was a serious problem with that idea: it's mid-April and the ice often leaves Moosehead Lake sometime in May. Of course depending on the spring weather, which was unusually warm that year, there could be an early "ice-out."

As we looked across the lake, we could see pools of water. However, from experience we knew, at least I did, that this was only standing water on top of the ice from the melting conditions. The big question was just how thick that ice was beneath that water.

It was then I came up with a brilliant idea—at least I convinced my wife it was brilliant. One of us would have to venture out onto the ice first, and the other would follow behind.

Now, common-sense told me that because my wife was much lighter, she should be the one to lead the way. I would tie a rope around her mid-section so if she went through the ice—a slim chance for a slim woman—I reasoned I could retrieve her with little problem. I convinced her that if we attempted this solution the other way around and I ended up in the lake, there was no way she could ever pull me out.

I realize this might sound foolhardy, but we tested the ice with a chisel every few feet and in most cases, it was still more than a foot thick. Still, for our friends across the ice who were watching the whole episode through field glasses, it was three hours of hilarious uninterrupted entertainment they said they would never forget.

You see, *they* knew there was absolutely no danger, as the ice was still safe to walk across. But *we* didn't know that and felt the need to be sure. So their watching the two of us was like watching a couple tiptoeing through a bed of tulips.

Our friends would later comment that all they could think of, or compare it with, was going to a county fair and watching a young farmer trying to team a twitch horse in a pulling ring.

After three-plus long hours, my loyal and brave wife and I made it safely across the ice, by this time totally exhausted—probably from all that tiptoeing through the tulips. Our legs were like rubber and they ached as if we had just climbed Mount Katahdin, Maine's highest peak.

Also, as we had made our way across the snowy melting ice, I had worn out my prized deer hide gloves and blistered both my hands from chopping through the ice to determine its thickness.

Although our friends drove us back to the mud-mired vehicle and helped pull us out, we had re-learned a valuable lesson: going to any camp on Moosehead Lake too early in the spring was okay, but you best plan on getting there by helicopter or by parachuting in.

Chapter 39

A Politician's Ideas and Philosophy

Most of the stories in this book are, for the most part, true. Oh, there may be an element of exaggeration now and then: poetic license they call it.

No license needed when talking about politicians, though. Even when you may not have first-hand knowledge of how a typical politician thinks, you'll surely recognize his ideas and philosophy here.

How would you like to have a politician, for example, who is also a close friend and wants a say in how you and your wife are handling your household finances? Let's take a look and see how things might work out. Keep in mind that up until now you're both doing fine on your own. In fact, you are salting a few bucks away each month.

Enter the politician friend, who might say, "Look folks, we've got to change a few things here in this household. You need to purchase a new car and take a well-deserved vacation. That used car is costing too much for repairs, and as for the vacation, you need to get away for a while to somewhere exotic."

The politician goes on. "I realize you have never lived beyond your means, but that's old-fashioned thinking, and that kind of thinking went away with the passing of your grandparents. Today it's different. Like in Washington and Augusta, forget where the money comes from and just do whatever you'd like and worry about the consequences later. Now that's the new way of thinking.

"Look, I venture to say that you folks probably don't have more than one or two credit cards. Bad idea!" he continued (you know how it goes once they get started). "Your wallet should be loaded with them. That way if you get a little short, you got a little something to fall back on by taking cash advances to carry you over. Good Lord, get enough of them and you'll never run out of money ever again."

My friend the politician went on for a while longer. As I said, "you know how it goes …."

"See," he said, "you only budget to eat out once a month. Heavens to Betsy, you folks must be bored to death. Come on, loosen up a little. Remember, do as we do in Washington and Augusta—spend it like you have it. That's the philosophy we've used in government for years. Look what it's done. Just for example, education. Why kids in public school now have a laptop of their own to use. You can't beat that now can you?"

The politician, who was becoming somewhat a more *distant* friend by the moment, couldn't seem to stop talking. Or, should I say, digging.

"Ah-ha! I see another one of your problems: You give too much to your church and charity. Let me tell you something that you may not know—your church and charities are much like the veterans who fought our wars. You need to give of course, but just enough to make it look good. That's how we handle things in Washington. That's why we keep the VA open in Togus: to save us money by not having to ship the vets to better facilities in other parts of the country. That's how we handle the vets. Oh, and the old folks, too. Besides, by us doing that we have more we can spend on the "pet projects" all of us get into politics for.

"Good idea, huh?" says my acquaintance and distant-friend politician. "Remember, squeeze the church and charities and you'll have more money for that vacation you'll be taking to the Bahamas."

Finally, I push a question in between his breathing. "But what if it doesn't work out and we really get in a financial bind?"

"Not to worry," he answers, "there is always the kids' college fund you can use. And remember I haven't even mentioned yet cashing in or taking out loans on your insurance policies."

My acquaintance and *very*-distant-friend politician turned to leave, trying to make his point a final time. "So once again, my final words to you are, spend it like you got it."

When the door finally closed, my wife and I decided to take the advice of our former friend and now acquaintance. We took some dough out of the cookie jar, saved by not having to make car payments, got into our used Chevy and headed to town for ice cream.

We both thought it might help us cool down.

Chapter 40
Sense & Sensibility

Over the years, many things have changed when it comes to social issues. In fact, I surmise that most people do not give much thought to these changes or, if they do, they do not say much about them.

I also believe some of those changes are good and for the better, while others are perhaps not so good, but neither are they bad—just seemingly unnecessary.

Doubtless, many of the changes—both in speech as well as physical actions—were good, necessary and beneficial to all when the civil rights movement was in full swing.

Yet, many of the so-called "politically correct" issues that followed are often bad as well as unnecessary. In fact, at first I wasn't sure that I knew for certain what this over-used phrase "politically correct" really meant anyway.

So the solution to this was to go to a trusted source, the dictionary. The first definition explained that "politically correct" meant: *"holding orthodox liberal political views usually used to denote dogmatism (or) excessive sensitivity to minority causes."*

Next I went to a Collegiate Dictionary and found a

slightly better definition: Political Correctness: n (1990) *conformity to a belief that language and practices which could offend political sensibilities should be eliminated. adj. (1936) conforming to a belief that language and practices which could offend political sensibilities (as in matters of sex or race should be eliminated.)*

Okay, so now we're getting somewhere. But these definitions still seemed awfully vague, especially with the magnitude of subject matters that now have this phrase connected to it.

A case in point: The word "squaw" has been part of our language since 1634, according to another newer dictionary (The American Heritage Dictionary). However, both college dictionaries define a "squaw" as: *a North American Indian woman or wife,* which is now considered offensive and therefore politically incorrect. I guess my question is, "How come it's taken 364 years for the last part of this definition (considered offensive) to come about?" I'm certainly no Ivy League scholar, but I'm no dummy, either.

Remember how a term or statement when used excessively is said to be "blank, blank something to death." When a former governor was feathering his cap to get laptop computers into the laps of every child of a certain age in every school in the state, he beat the subject matter of laptops to death.

Okay, I'm sure you're getting my drift here that we are Politically Correcting and In-correcting ourselves to death. I ask, "When this overused term is used, what and who is behind the change or who and what benefits from it being changed?" Case in point is the change just described above. Certainly I get no benefit from the change. In fact, most people I know get no benefit from it.

Further think of the money that it must cost state taxpayers to make this change. In addition, I venture to say there isn't one car in 100 that passes the sign in Greenville that reads Squaw Mountain and comments: *"Did you see that sign we just passed? It called that mountain Squaw. That's terrible!"*

What happened to the free speech philosophy? You know, the First Amendment of the U.S. Constitution that guarantees free speech? It just seems those people intent on making sure everything is PC, are also strong advocates of free speech.

You cannot have it both ways.

So, with this all said, I think a person can govern himself or herself anyway they see fit as long as it is within the law. But others should not force, or try to force, their ideas, beliefs, religion, convictions and political correctness on the majority who may think differently.

I use the word "force" because if you are in the minority for any one of a thousand reasons and want to change my mind or point of view to your ideas or philosophies, you are free to do it.

So am I free to listen or not. But in a democracy we live under the law of majority rule—or so I thought.

Finally, I would point out it just seems that today all anyone with a personal cause or "ax to grind" has to do is invoke the phrase "political incorrect" and they are on their way for the change they are advocating.

Come to think about it, why don't I hitch a ride on this bandwagon? All right everyone . . . from now on no one calls me Blubber-Gut again!

Chapter 41

The Agreeable Farmer with the Unlucky Pig

It seems a couple of hunters wanted to go hunting on this farmer's land, but to get to his wooded area they had to cross this rather large field. Being good, considerate hunters, they thought it best to get permission from the farmer.

They found the farmer working on his woodpile and proceeded to ask permission to hunt on his land. The farmer agreed but added, "Be vry caful whn ya cross ta tha field down thea cuz thesa aful big hole bout midway."

The two assured the farmer they would be careful, then thanked him and went on their way. Sure enough midway across the field they came upon this monstrous hole. Not only was it big it was also deep. "Boy that's a deep hole" one hunter said to the other.

"Yeah, it sure is, I wonder how deep it is?"

With that said, they proceed to the wooded area where they were going to hunt.

They hadn't gone but a short distance when they came upon a big ole truck transmission. "Huh" one hunter gestured to the other, "You know, if we were to drop that down that hole, we'd know how deep it was when it hit bottom."

"Good idea," the other said.

As they labored getting the transmission to the hole, they finally rolled it in. About the same time that the transmission was on its way to the bottom, they looked up and saw this pig coming on the dead run right for them. Now it was obvious if they didn't get out of the way this pig was going to run them over. As they both leaped to opposite sides of the hole the pig fell straight into it.

"Did you see that," one asked the other. "We better go tell the farmer his pig just fell in that hole."

"Good idea; lets go," the other agreed.

They found the farmer again at his woodpile and as they excitedly told the farmer about the pig falling in the hole, the farmer nearly went berserk. "Impossible," the farmer declared with assertion. "Thars no way that thar pig couda fell in that thar hole . . . I had him tied to a big transmissun."

Chapter 42

The Story of Walt

As I've stated before, "Friends come in all sizes, colors, shapes and ages. Some are close; some are distant. Some are best friends, while others are dear. If we're lucky they are both dear and best." Well, Walt fit most of those words to a "T." He stood 6' 4" and carried his 225 pound like a well-trained football player. Walt was not only a close friend, but a dear and best friend as well.

Walt and I go back to the late 1940s and early 1950s when we went to two different schools and competed in athletics against one another. I guess I would be less than honest to pretend that we were even friends of any kind back then. Visualize if you will, standing in the batters box at a mere 5' 9 and this 200+ lb. 6' 4' giant throwing a ball at you probably going in excess of 80 or 90 miles an hour, or trying to make a basket on the basket ball court with this "incredible hulk" of a kid standing over you. It was pretty hard to even like this guy back then. In fact the only emotion that fit back then was—we all dreaded to see him coming to compete against us.

Thank goodness those emotions of dread and fear

changed as we grew older and both graduated from our respective schools; perhaps not even then, but certainly when we both returned from the army back in 1955. Although it is somewhat unclear just how this wonderful friendship started, it may have begun at a Maine sponsored trade school called SMVTI (Southern Maine Vocational Technical Institute). We both enrolled there after we were discharged from the army. Walt chose the IE (Industrial Electricity) course, and I the MST (Machine Shop Technology).

It was here that our friendship flourished as we spent a lot of off time together. I was going through a painful divorce and Walt was there to pick up the pieces. Some weekends we spent traveling to North Andover, Massachusetts to visit his sister, and others were spent doing our own individual thing. The friendship grew to one of mutual respect for one another and we became best of friends.

After two years (in 1957), we both graduated and went back to our respective homes. That is to say, Walt went back to his home-farm in New Sharon, and I, well let's just say I went back to "whence I came." However, I ended up staying at Walt's farm in New Sharon. It is here where that best friend turned into a dear friend. We began fishing together and somehow acquired a mutual friend and his wife, who turned out to be dear friends to both of us.

We would travel to remote fishing spots sometimes walking seven miles to reach our destination; however once there, the fishing for brook trout was an absolute paradise. In addition, that friendship provided many other experiences, some of which would be better served if left to the reader's imagination. Let's just say . . . doing what young men in their early 20s do when there is no parental supervision.

Then we both found love, and low and behold, Walt chose and honored me with the distinction of being best man at his wedding to a beautiful and wonderful girl named Jane. Their marriage—to date—has spanned more than 50 years. From there, it was a continued friendship one finds very rarely in a lifetime. A variety of different jobs and job locations would separate us for periods of time, yet eventually that friendship found us back together again.

Once more there were fishing trips and family gatherings. Then for some unknown reason, although the friendship never ended, the contact with one another did. This would last for twenty-six long years with absolutely no animosity toward one another, just no physical contact. As for me, the thoughts of Walt and Jane were always there. Hopefully the same can be said of them, yet no contact was made by either.

Then in January of 2011, I found a telephone message on my answering machine; it was Walt. With shaky hands I returned the call, and arranged to meet at my home the following week. I don't have the necessary vocabulary to express my sincere thanks, not only for that phone call, but for that wonderful visit with Walt.

It was wall to wall reminiscing with promises of other visits in the near future.

Finally it was time for Walt to leave for home. Even though our visit had lasted through lunch and beyond, the time was too short. I, in that short span of time that day, suddenly began to realize just how valuable that friendship was. As Walt's car left my driveway tears streamed from my eyes into my nearly white beard.

My feelings were ambiguous: ashamed about our lack of contact for the past 26 years, yet thankful that we finally reconnected. After all, we *were*, and still *are*, best friends.

Chapter 43

No One Will Be Forgotten

It goes without saying that when one devotes a part his life to meeting interesting people, then makes a point to record some of those meetings, there will be many stories to tell.

It would seem that so far this has held true for me. But what about all of those other folks I have met, and their stories that did not make the pages of this book? Surely they had worthwhile stories that also would have been interesting to read about.

Although that last statement is absolutely true, there are some stories that must remain untold. Are those stories any less interesting than those included in this anthology? Absolutely not. In fact, some of the stories left out may be more interesting than the ones left in.

For example, there are stories of a truly dear and loyal friend and old Army buddy, who lives in Florida, that would make for outstanding reading. This is to say that here was a guy who was the only one of a total of 240 other men (including myself) that received a weekend pass for his meticulous and innovative way he cleaned his rifle.

Or stories about two twin uncles, who I worked

for in my younger years, which would be of interest to many. And what made these twin uncles so special? Well, lots of things; but perhaps most of all, they invented the plastic coated bowling pin that received the first American Bowling Congress (ABC) seal of approval for the (then up-and-coming) automatic pinsetter. This story would also include a son of one of the twin uncles who saved me from a possible 20-year visit to an army brig by answering morning revile muster while I went AWOL to get married to his childhood sweetheart.

Then there is this great guy in New York who was the most dedicated employee and friend a person could have until his death a few years ago.

The same can be said of another fellow from New York who wasn't an employee but a business partner for many years. Our trials and tribulations were certainly worthy of more than a brief story in this book. Incidentally this fellow, a graduate from Rensselaer Polytechnic Institute, was an engineer for the Singer Sewing Machine Company in his younger years and was instrumental in developing the zigzag attachment for the company. He would be the most creative engineer I would ever know in my lifetime. In my association with him, he co-invented, and we co-built, the first automated bowling ball drilling machine for sports shops and bowling alleys.

There are many more examples that could be cited here. However, all of those mentioned and the others that could be recorded are all from states other than Maine. This fact certainly does not diminish their importance or in anyway indicate that their stories were not of great importance to me. In addition, the stories that could be told about these truly valued folks are surely subject matter for another time, another place, and another book.

The intent of this book was to demonstrate exclusively, not only a bit of Yankee ingenuity, but some of the humor in exercising that Yankee trait. Therefore, only characters from Maine have been used. Hopefully, there will be no one slighted by this approach, and the stories chosen will serve the intended purpose of this book.

I already realize I have left out many interesting characters and stories, but I think I will save them for another volume. I hope the people I have described in these vignettes, as well as those who will have to wait for the second installment, understand and enjoy the book just the same.

I certainly enjoyed writing it, and remembering the countless characters and experiences that have so enriched my life.

***A final true story of one of
Strong's most beloved Characters***

Chapter 44

Roy Lewis' Drug Store

If you had ten cents, you could sit upon a stool at the marble counter of Roy Lewis' Drug Store in Strong, Maine and have an ice cream with butterscotch sauce and chocolate sprills. Roy Lewis made his own ice cream and everyone remembers it being the very best.

You could put a penny into a machine, pull down a lever, and out would come a hand full of Spanish peanuts. Five-cent candy bars were very large compared to today's standard bars. Remember the large Milky Ways, Forever Yours, Peppermint Patties, and a large block of molasses's honeycomb candy, each for the price of a nickel? Then there was a showcase of many kinds of chocolates displayed on trays with a label on the front of each telling their flavors. The little "Opera Creams" would melt in your mouth. There was a tall, pointed chocolate with a vanilla center called "Cheap Chocolates." These were less expensive.

Roy Lewis was good at doctoring. If there wasn't a licensed doctor available, he would suggest something that would help the problem. He would mix up a solution that would take the dryness from your hands and make the cracks disappear like magic.

He loved children and liked to entertain them. When they came through the door, he'd grab a horn and start to blow it . . . or wind up some toy to get a child's interest. He got as much fun out of it as they did.

Roy was also a photographer and took pictures of the town and its people and put them on postcards. These were displayed on swivel metal racks to be sold for five cents.

During the Christmas season, the store was a magical place for young children. They all knew how everything worked and had a chance to "try out" all of the toys before the 25th of December. It probably helped his business, but also gave him a chance to perform and give of himself to others.

This was a part of Strong to remember. How could anyone forget the good things to eat, the toys, Roy the druggist, and his wife Mabel, who worked alongside her husband in this popular and vital town pharmacy.

* * * * * *

Here are a few more facts and information about the wonderful druggist, husband, and town servant, taken from the *"Strong, Maine—Incorporated 1801"* historical book, pages 181 and 182.

Lester Royal "Roy" and Mabel Smith Lewis

Roy Lewis was born in Auburn in 1889 and came to Strong at the age of two. His family moved to an apartment over the storehouse of Burnham and Morrill's Corn Factory, where his father was in charge of operations.

At age 24 Roy took a position in the drug store operated by another man, Mr. Charles Dyer, and Roy worked as an apprentice for him for 24 years. When Mr. Dyer died, Roy bought the drug store and studied diligently to get certified as a registered druggist.

This business provided the opportunity for Roy to serve the people of Strong for his entire life; all that knew him respected him beyond words.

With his wife Mabel by his side throughout the years, their drug store provided not only a soda fountain but homemade ice cream as well. In fact, people from miles around would travel long distances just to get this ice cream.

However this was not just a drug store as it often carried many items, even wallpaper. Although Roy and Mabel operated the drug store for 25 years, they only took one vacation during a 30-year period.

On pages 182 through 183 of *"Strong, Maine— Incorporated 1801"* are paragraph after paragraph of Roy Lewis's accomplishments and his untiring dedication to everything that was part of his life that you may wish to read.

* * * * * *

So what was it about Roy Lewis that made him such a "character," but in a different sense than the other story-characters portrayed in this book?

Well, many things.

First, Roy was never without either a smile on his face, a whistle coming from his lips, or a tune coming from his mouth. I never saw Roy Lewis angry or out of sorts. Roy was not only a gentleman; he was a gentle man.

He was also one who had a deep and dedicated involvement in his church and several other town affairs. For years Roy played the trombone in the town band. His musical talent was extraordinary; he even sang in the church choir for many years.

Yes, without a doubt Roy Lewis was a "character," and a lovable one who had no equal. My memories of Roy will never be forgotten, as he was, after all, a part of my life too. Perhaps most importantly of all, Roy represented what it took to be a gentle man with a big heart, who touched the lives of so many, and most certainly, of all those that knew him as their trusted druggist.

Lester Roy Lewis' Drug Store
Strong, Maine

Customer Mike Melanson, with his purchase
Mabel Lewis and L. Roy Lewis
behind the counter

* * * * * *

This concludes my stories about characters in Strong and other small towns in Maine. When I began this project, my intent was to devote some pages to social issues. However, with so much "doom and gloom" already in our lives today, those thoughts and plans were changed to relating jokes and tall tales, hoping to give joy and cheerfulness instead.

I would like to end this book with one more funny story, that came from the very last page of the historical society's book, *"Strong, Maine—Incorporated 1801."* Enjoy . . . .

Chapter 45

The Potato Digger

One day many years ago, a gentleman farmer stopped into the local hardware store to purchase a potato digger. As he explained to the storeowner, he had either mislaid his or someone had borrowed it, so guess he'd buy a new one.

"Good" the storeowner replied as he took one off the rack and laid it on the counter.

After their usual conversations of how to save the world, it got time for the farmer to get back to diggin' his potatoes. "How much will that be?" the farmer asked.

"Dollar an' a quarter," came the reply.

"What?" the farmer responded. "Why I can buy one at Sears Roebuck for a dollar."

"Tell you what," the storeowner fired back "If Sears Roebuck will sell you one for a dollar; I'll sell you one for a dollar."

With that said the farmer laid the dollar on the counter and proceeded to take the potato digger and walk off. "Hold on a minute," the storeowner demanded. "That'll be another quarter."

"Whaddya mean another quarter? You said you'd sell it to me for the same price as Sears Roebuck."

"And I have," the storeowner says. Then he continues, "The postage to get it here is going to cost another quarter, right?"

The farmer reluctantly responds, "Okay, you got me on that one," and puts another quarter down on the counter to go with the dollar.

After talking a few more minutes, the farmer then decides he must be going and he reaches to pick up the potato digger. However, the storeowner already has it in his grasp and puts it under the counter. "What's goin' on here?" the farmer says "I've paid a quarter more than I would have to pay at Sears Roebuck."

. . . Before the farmer can say anything further, the storekeeper responds, "Since this is a Sears Roebuck deal, that digger won't be here for another three or four days."

About the Author

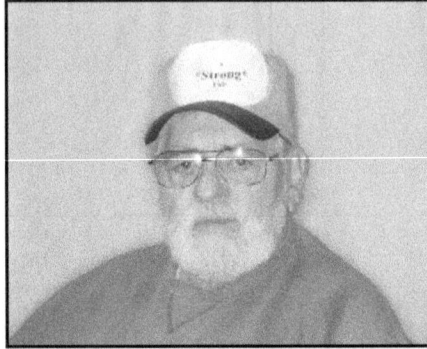

People write books for a multitude of reasons. The author of this book of short stories and tall tales had just one purpose in mind when he began writing. Before we learn more about this author and why he started to write, he should be identified. To friends, neighbors and other acquaintances, he is known as Richard A. Bean, with a nickname of Dick or Beany.

So, why did Dick start writing? To rehabilitate an injured and damaged brain he received working as a private contractor in a paper mill. A brain injury caused by the ingestion of highly toxic substances (chemicals and gases) working in the most dangerous and polluted section of this mill.

When no help could be obtained from the medical, legal, or his workmen's compensation insurance to help rehabilitate his damaged brain, he undertook the task himself, beginning with his writing.

Although the stories may be less than perfect, most are true as he recalls them. Fortunately the brain damage did not affect the recall of distant events in spite of the fact his short-term memory, which was once nearly photographic, diminished to being practically non-existent. So, what initially was started to rehabilitate his injured brain hopefully has developed into something that can be enjoyed by all.

Richard A. (Dick) Bean Sr.

www.ingramcontent.com/pod-product-compliance
Lightning Source LLC
LaVergne TN
LVHW051626080426
835511LV00016B/2205